BEYOND THE

HORIZON

BEYOND THE HORIZON

A Journey of Self-Discovery

BLAIR LINDSAY

BEYOND THE HORIZON
© 2025 Blair Lindsay. All rights reserved.

For rights and permissions, please contact:

Blair Lindsay

blairdigital33@gmail.com
@TheBLindsay on X
@theblindsay on Instagram
www.blairlindsay5.wordpress.com

A NOTE FROM BLAIR...

This book began as a way to process the past four years of my life—years that have been shaped by the world-changing events of COVID-19 and the deeply personal impact it had on my mental health. At 23, I look back at those turbulent times and feel an overwhelming need to share the story, not just as my own, but as one that could resonate with others navigating similar struggles. Though told through the eyes of a fictional character named Louis, much of the narrative is grounded in real events, emotions, and reflections from my own life.

The challenges Louis faces—depression, questioning his identity, navigating relationships, and seeking a sense of belonging—are rooted in my own journey. But through Louis, I've found a way to explore universal themes of acceptance, sexuality, and ultimately, the search for one's calling in a world that often feels isolating.

Writing this book has been a cathartic and transformative experience. It's allowed me to confront my past, embrace my vulnerabilities, and hopefully, offer a sense of connection to anyone who reads it. If Louis's story resonates with even one person, then the struggle and the writing will have been worth it. I hope this book reminds you that no matter how difficult life gets, there is always room for growth, self-acceptance, and the possibility of finding your path in this ever-changing world.

Yours,

Blair x

For my Mum and Gran, my unwavering pillars of support—thank you for guiding me, believing in me, and filling my life with love. To my late Gran, who showed me such kindness and compassion, I hope this makes you proud. To my Aunt L, for kickstarting my love of reading by gifting me books every birthday and Christmas, nurturing a passion that has shaped my life. To my English teachers, Mrs McCrone, Mrs Melson, and Mrs Naismith, for encouraging my storytelling, even when the words were only whispers on a page. To my best friend, for standing by me through everything, and to my friends who walked beside me through the darkest chapters and gave me the strength to keep going—I am forever grateful. To my Dad, for showing me that it's never too late to rebuild bridges, and to my brothers and the bond we'll always share – no matter what. To my childhood dog, whose loyal companionship I carry in my heart, and my two cats, Hope and Binx, for their comforting mischief and endless reminders of joy. This book is a tribute to all of you, for helping me see what lies beyond the horizon.

CONTENTS

PROLOGUE

SEVENTEENS FINAL BREATHS

The night before his eighteenth birthday, Louis lay awake, staring at the ceiling, listening to the rain tapping against his window. The room was dark, but his mind was wide awake, restless with thoughts he could not quite shape into words.

Eighteen. It was supposed to mean something. A milestone. A threshold into adulthood. But instead of excitement, all he felt was the weight of everything he had not figured out yet.

He turned onto his side, the soft glow of his phone screen illuminating his face. A few birthday messages had already come through, warm words that should have made him feel something more. He typed out a response, fingers hesitating over the keyboard before sending something casual, something that did not reveal the knots twisting in his stomach.

His eyes flickered to the framed photo on his bedside table. A much younger version of himself grinned up at the camera, standing beside his Dad at an old Glasgow police box, much like the TARDIS from Doctor Who. The memory felt like a different lifetime. He wondered if his Dad would call tomorrow. If he would remember.

A deep sigh escaped his lips as he turned onto his back again, staring into the dark. It wasn't just his Dad. It was everything. His future. His place in the world. Who he was meant to be.

Eighteen was supposed to feel like freedom, but all Louis felt was uncertainty.

Still, the morning would come, whether he was ready for it or not.

And maybe—just maybe—this would be the year he finally figured things out.

CHAPTER ONE
THE WEIGHT OF EIGHTEEN

"Thanks, Mum. I love it." Louis held up the Fred Perry jumper, the fabric soft and fresh beneath his fingers. A grin tugged at his lips, though some of him felt the moment's weight.

"You can wear it tonight," his Mum replied, her blue eyes—so much like his own—lighting up. "Eighteen, Louis. You've got such a bright future ahead of you."

Her words were full of hope, but they landed with an unexpected heaviness. Eighteen. The number seemed too big, too heavy for someone who still found comfort in old routines and memories of Saturday nights spent watching Doctor Who with his Dad. But he forced a smile and nodded.

"Yeah. I hope so."

The living room glowed warmly in the afternoon light. Two silver balloons floated near the dining table, their numbers glinting: 1 and 8. A chocolate cake sat nearby, its candles waiting for the evening's celebration. Mika, their ageing terrier, dozed in her usual spot by the fireplace, occasionally twitching her paws in a dream.

"Gran will be over soon," his Mum added, folding the gift wrap into neat squares. "We'll take some pictures before you head out."

Louis's phone buzzed on the arm of the couch. A message from his friend Carly:

Are you ready to paint the town red?

He smiled to himself, typing back a quick reply:

Always.

Upstairs, the floorboards creaked as he moved toward the bathroom. He caught his reflection in the mirror—tousled brown hair, a diamond stud glinting in his left ear. He straightened his posture, standing six feet tall, but the confidence felt hollow. The truth was that Louis was not sure he was ready for the weight of being an adult.

Later, freshly dressed and standing at the bus stop, he felt the crispness of his new jumper against his skin. – keeping him warm from the cold January air. Mika had followed him to the gate, her tail wagging as she watched him leave.

"See you later, girl," he murmured, crouching to scratch her ears. Her bright eyes held his gaze as if she understood more than she let on.

The bus ride into town was uneventful but comforting in its routine. The hum of the engine, the muted chatter of passengers, and the occasional ding of the stop bell created a familiar backdrop. By the time he reached his usual hairdresser, Louis felt more like himself.

"Just a number two on the back and sides, and take a bit off the top," he instructed the stylist.

16

"Big plans tonight?" she asked, expertly wielding the clippers.

"Heading to Glasgow with a friend. Birthday night out."

"Well, happy birthday!" she said with a smile. "Eighteen, right? The world's your oyster."

Louis chuckled. "That's the plan."

Back home, his Gran's arrival brought warmth and laughter. She handed him a small blue gift bag and a card, her smile as bright as ever. Inside was a crisp fifty-pound note and a bottle of Hugo Boss aftershave.

"Just a little something to treat yourself," she said as Louis beamed.

"Thanks, Gran" he replied, before pulling her into a warm embrace.

Then from the kitchen doorway, his Mum appeared, carrying the birthday cake. The candles flickered, casting a warm glow across her face as she sang 'Happy Birthday'.

Louis leaned forward, closing his eyes briefly before blowing them out. *I wish for something more.*

Later that evening, Carly was waiting at the station. Her tall, slender frame and easy grin made her a magnetic presence.

"Nice jumper," she teased, nodding toward his new Fred Perry. "Birthday gift?"

"You know it," Louis replied, gesturing to the Nike trainers he had bought earlier. "Treating myself."

17

Together, they bought tickets and passed the time watching TikToks, their laughter blending into the station's hum. On the train to Glasgow, Louis checked his phone. Messages flooded in from friends and family, but one notification made his chest flutter—a DM from Paul, a guy he had been chatting with on Instagram for weeks:

Happy birthday, cutie. I hope it's a good one for you!

Louis's fingers hovered before he typed back:

Thanks, Paul. You just made my day.

Tucking his phone away, Louis gazed out the window at the countryside rushing past, trying to shake the ache of his Dad's silence.

"Not even a message," he murmured to Carly as they waited for the train. His voice was low as if saying it aloud made the truth too real.

She frowned, her usual teasing expression softening. "Forget him. Tonight's about you."

But Louis could not forget. The silence from Dad was deafening. Every buzz of his phone from friends and family wishing him well felt hollow without the one message he secretly longed for.

Birthdays were not always like this. He could still remember the card Dad would write every year, the way his name would appear in his Dad's sharp, slanted handwriting. Back then, the words *"love, Dad"* at the end had felt unshakable, a foundation that could hold anything. Now, they were just an echo.

The ache followed him like a shadow. Even as Carly pulled him into laughter over TikToks and the buzz of the train filled the air, the weight of the unspoken loomed large. When the city lights of Glasgow came into view, they did not ignite the kind of excitement they once had. Instead, they reflected the questions spinning in his mind: *Why didn't he care enough? What had gone so wrong? Was it something about me?*

At TGI Fridays, Louis fell into the joy Carly worked so hard to create. He smiled as the servers cheered and brought out a surprise slice of cake, his name spelt in icing. Yet, as everyone sang, his eyes briefly flicked to his phone again. The screen was blank.

By the time they walked along the River Clyde, the frigid air bit at his cheeks, but it wasn't enough to shake the dull ache in his chest. He stopped by the railing, gazing at the city lights shimmering in the water.

"I know it's stupid to care," he said, voice heavy, breaking the comfortable silence between them. "I mean, it has been years. I should be used to it by now, right?"

Carly sighed, stepping closer. "It is not stupid, Louis. He is your Dad. It's okay to want him to show up for you."

Louis let the words settle, his gaze fixed on the dark water below. "I just thought maybe... just one text, you know?"

Carly didn't reply immediately. She placed a hand on his shoulder, grounding him. Her presence was steady, unyielding, the kind of support that did not need words.

19

As they continued walking, Louis tried to push the thoughts aside, but the absence of his Dad's voice lingered. He felt its weight in every laugh, every moment of joy. The night was meant to celebrate him, but a part of him could not stop mourning what was missing.

"I'm happy we did this," he said softly.

Carly smiled; her warmth unwavering. "Me too. This day is all about you, Louis. And we made it one to remember."

But as they walked along the riverbank, his thoughts strayed to the complexities waiting for him beyond this night—questions of identity, ambition, and belonging. He let them rest for now, focusing instead on the steady comfort of Carly's friendship and the bright horizon ahead.

Louis awoke to Mika's eager face nuzzling against his cheek, her warm tongue pulling him out of sleep. His thoughts drifted to last week's birthday celebration—a day filled with family, his dearest friend, and the rare freedom to feel genuinely himself. He smiled, remembering Carly's unstoppable energy. The moment he had blown out the candles on his cake felt incredibly vivid, the wish he had made still lingering in his heart.

After a quick shower, Louis tucked into a breakfast of toast and jam before slipping on his favourite Fred Perry jumper—a gift from his Mum on the big day. Catching his reflection in the mirror, he paused, spritzing the warm, familiar scent of aftershave his Gran had given him. It felt like a quiet armour against the day ahead, one he was determined to fill with purpose. He grabbed his bag and set off for his college campus.

The January chill was sharp, but the lively hum of students swapping stories and ideas on Glasgow College's grounds warmed the air. Inside his radio classroom, desks formed a semi-circle around microphones and computers, creativity buzzing like static.

"Hey, Louis! Ready to put it all together?" Megan asked, her rocker vibes on full display with a vintage band tee and messy red hair pulled into a high ponytail.

"Absolutely," he replied, sliding into his seat. "I'm editing my interview with Fourth Daughter today."

"Nice! Cannot wait to hear it." Megan grinned as she adjusted her setup.

As Louis began piecing together his project, a familiar unease gnawed at him. It had been a week since his birthday, and still not a single word from his Dad. The silence, heavier with every passing day, made the memory of the celebration bittersweet.

Megan noticed his distraction. "You good?" she asked, her voice tinged with concern.

"Yeah, just… thinking about my Dad," Louis admitted, fiddling with his headphones. "He didn't even text me last week."

Megan frowned. "Seriously? Not even a 'Happy Birthday'?"

He shook his head, a bitter laugh escaping. "Nope. I shouldn't be surprised anymore, but it still hurts?"

Megan placed a hand on his arm. "That's rough, Lou. You don't deserve that."

"And what would be the point of me reaching out to him? He only talks to me when it suits him," Louis muttered, frustration tightening his voice. "I'm just tired of feeling like an afterthought."

The weight of his words hung between them, but Megan gave him a reassuring nudge. "You deserve better. Don't let him dim your shine, okay? You've got way too much going for you."

Her words settled into him as he turned his attention back to his project. The familiar editing rhythm soon drew him in, piecing together the artist's thoughtful insights with his commentary. As the final segment came together, a swell of pride pushed aside the lingering ache in his chest.

After class, as he packed up, a familiar voice called out from the hallway.

"Hey, Louis!" Sarah -an old school friend- called out, her long blonde hair cascading over her shoulders. Dressed in a cosy white jumper and jeans, she exuded effortless warmth.

"Sarah! It's been ages," Louis said, his grin widening as he left the classroom, and they headed off campus together.

As they headed towards the bus stop, they chatted about old times and caught up on each other's lives.

"Now that your 'legal' fancy coming out this weekend?" Sarah asked, her eyes sparkling with excitement.

"Definitely. Who's in?"

"Everyone! I'll make a group chat. First Ed, then Baker's. It will be great to get us all back together again" she said, her enthusiasm contagious.

"For sure, I'll text Carly. I've missed our nights together," Louis replied, already feeling excited about reuniting with his friends.

When they reached the bus stop, the conversation shifted.

"Been talking to anyone lately?" Sarah teased, raising an eyebrow.

Louis chuckled, a blush creeping onto his cheeks. "A few guys here and there, but it is mostly just one-time things."

Sarah nodded knowingly. "Tell me about it! It's like everyone is looking for a hookup, it's hard to find something real."

"Exactly," Louis said with a sigh. "Sometimes I just want a connection, you know? Not something shallow."

As their bus pulled up, Louis's thoughts turned to Paul. They had only been messaging for a few weeks, but their conversations were different—genuine and unforced. He hadn't told Sarah about Paul yet; it felt too delicate, too important. Besides, Paul wasn't 'out of the closet,' and Louis respected his privacy.

They found seats at the back of the bus, and Sarah held out her pinkie finger with a grin. "Let's make this weekend about us—no boys, no drama."

"Deal," Louis said, locking his pinkie with hers.

Their laughter filled the bus as they reminisced about old sleepovers and ridiculous adventures. Sitting beside Sarah, Louis felt a sense of hope settle in his chest. Being with his old school friend, reminded him of everything he still had—friends, dreams, and days of joy worth chasing. And for the first time in a while, the future did not seem so far away.

The streetlights cast long shadows across the pavement as Louis got off the bus and walked home. Mika's excited barking greeted him as soon as he opened the door. She bounded toward him, her wiry tail wagging furiously.

"Hey, girl," he said, crouching down to let her lick his face. "Miss me?"

His Mum appeared in the doorway; her apron dusted with flour. "Just in time! Dinner's almost ready. How was your day?"

"Good," he replied, shrugging off his coat. "Sarah says hi."

His Mum smiled knowingly. "Aw good! I'm glad you two are in touch again. She's a good friend."

Louis nodded, following the comforting smell of home-cooked lasagna into the kitchen.

They sat at the dinner table, dinner was warm and familiar, and their laughter blended into the soft hum of the radio playing in the background. Yet, as they talked about their day, Louis couldn't help but glance at his phone. The silence from his Dad still lingered, an unwelcome guest at the table.

Later, as he lay in bed, Mika curled up on his stomach; Louis stared at the glow of his screen. The messages from Sarah, Carly, and his friends in the group chat - filled him with gratitude, but still, the absence of his Dad's name cut deep.

He drafted a message to his Dad, his fingers hesitating over the keys. He wanted to say so much—to ask why, to tell him how much.

It hurt—but no words felt right. Deleting the draft, he placed the phone on his bedside table and turned off the light.

Mika's steady breathing filled the quiet as the room sank into darkness. Louis reached down to gently scratch behind her ears, finding comfort in her presence. The ache in his chest had not disappeared, but tonight, he let the thought of Saturday, catching up with old friends- carry him forward. And for now, that was *enough*.

Saturday night arrived, buzzing with an energy that mirrored Louis's excitement for the night ahead. He had been texting the group chats all morning, finalizing the plans. Each ping of his phone heightened his anticipation—tonight was about friendship, fun, and escaping his worries.

After a quick shower, Louis slipped into a fitted black shirt and his favourite Nike shoes and carefully styled his hair. The familiar scent of his Hugo Boss aftershave lingered on his skin, offering comfort and warmth as he headed out.

He met his friends at their first stop of the night, First Edition. They quickly found a cosy booth and slipped into their old rhythm of easy banter and inside jokes.

"Who's ready for some shots?" Carly's eyes glinted with mischief as she raised her glass.

"Just one!" Louis laughed, raising his hand in mock surrender. "Gotta pace myself for the club later."

As the drinks kept flowing, so did their conversations, talking about their school days, weekend sleepovers, and the time they had all gone to Blackpool together.

"What was it you would shout every time we were on a ride at Pleasure Beach Louis?" Sarah asked.

"When in Rome?" Louis questioned.

"No, it was someone's name, what was it!" Sarah replied, eagerly tapping the table trying to think.

"CHARLENE!" Carly yelled out, loud enough that everyone in the pub would have heard her.

"YES, that was it!" Sarah replied, "Who even was Charlene?" She continued.

Louis laughed. "I have no idea, but we found it funny at the time."

"Anyway, what's next after this? Are we still going to Baker's?" Carly asked.

"Definitely! I Heard the new DJ's a blast," Karen piped in. Short with curly brown hair, Karen's contagious energy always lit up the room. She had that way of pulling everyone in with her lively spirit.

Beside her sat Lauren, quieter but no less present. Lauren's sleek black hair framed her fair face, and though she didn't speak much, her subtle humour and warm smile made her a constant in their circle.

Louis felt the adrenaline surge. The thought of hitting the dance floor and losing himself in the music was exactly what he needed tonight. After their drinks, they ventured into the crisp night air, heading toward the club.

Inside, the atmosphere was electric—a whirlwind of flashing lights, booming bass, and the heat of the crowd. Louis felt his heart race as they found a booth near the dance floor. The music quickly overtook him, as he got up on the floor and lost himself in the rhythm.

As the night wore on, they danced, laughed, and sang together, their voices blending with the crowd. After a few songs, they broke for drinks. Louis ordered another round of shots.

"Here's to us!" he shouted, barely audible over the music. "And to friendship!"

"To friendship!" they echoed, clinking glasses before diving back into the music.

But then Sarah leaned in, her tone serious despite the lightness of the toast. "Remember our promise? No boys tonight?"

Louis smirked. "I remember. Just us."

"Good," Sarah teased.

The group laughed, danced, and sang some more. Sarah and Louis twirled together on the dance floor, their friends egging them on to do the 'lift scene' from Dirty Dancing. The promise they'd made earlier in the night still lingered, though it began to feel more distant as the drinks kept coming, and the night unfolded. Louis had noticed a few guys around them, but his focus remained on the people and the joy of the evening.

Back at their booth, Carly's eyes lit up with mischievous excitement. "Have you heard the latest news?"

Karen raised an eyebrow. "Another one of Carly's conspiracy theories?"

"No, seriously!" Carly leaned in. "Did you hear about that virus spreading in China? It's from someone eating a bat or something. It's all over the news."

Louis raised an eyebrow. "A bat? That sounds like a horror movie."

"I read about it earlier today," Carly continued. "People are freaking out. They say it might even spread to the UK soon."

Karen pretended to shudder. "Imagine being stuck indoors for weeks because of some bat-eating virus."

Louis chuckled, shaking his head. "No way. We're tougher than that."

Carly lifted her glass. "Well, here's to living our best lives before any virus ruins it!"

They clinked glasses, dismissing the news as another bizarre headline. The music called them back to the dance floor and worries about the outside world soon faded into the background.

Just then, out of the corner of his eye, Louis spotted Paul. Standing by the bar, tall and striking with blonde hair, his smile pulled Louis in. Their eyes met, and Louis's heart skipped a beat. He hadn't expected to see him here.

Just as he was about to consider walking away, his phone buzzed with a DM from Paul:

Hey you! Follow me over here.

Louis glanced at Sarah, who was dancing with Carly. Quietly, he slipped away, curiosity propelling him forward. What harm could there be in seeing where this spark might lead?

Paul leaned against a wall with a sly smirk outside a dimly lit bathroom. He nodded towards the bathroom "Just for a minute?" he whispered, his voice low.

Louis nodded as they stepped inside, the sounds of the club became muffled. Paul's presence was magnetic, and Louis's breath caught in his throat as he moved closer.

"I'm happy we've finally met tonight," Paul whispered, his lips brushing against Louis's ear.

Louis nodded, his heart racing. The anticipation had been building for weeks, and now that they were face to face, everything felt charged with possibility.

Without another word, Paul leaned in, and their lips met softly at first, then deepened into something more passionate and electric. Louis melted into the kiss, his heart hammering as Paul's hand found his waist, pulling him closer.

For a split second, everything else disappeared—the music, the crowd, the noise. There was only Paul and Louis and the spark between them.

When they pulled apart, breathless, Paul smiled, but the look in his eyes shifted. "I should get back to my friends," he said, glancing around the club. "See you later?"

Louis nodded, his heart still racing, trying to steady himself. "Yeah, sure."

Paul hesitated, his gaze flickering with something Louis could not quite place. "And maybe… don't tell anyone about this. I've been chatting to your friend Sarah."

Louis's stomach dropped. The thrill of the kiss evaporated, replaced by confusion and frustration. Paul was seeing Sarah. That hadn't crossed his mind -not once- why would it? And now, it felt like a punch to the gut.

"Right," Louis managed to say, forcing a smile that felt brittle. "Of course."

Paul left, and Louis stood there, the taste of the kiss lingering on his lips, mixing with the bitterness of Paul's words. He felt something—a mix of betrayal and anger—gnawing at him. How could Paul lead him on like this? And more than that, why had Paul kept his budding romance with Sarah hidden from him?

The weight of it all started to settle in. He hadn't expected to feel this way—he had just wanted a taste of something real, something more than the shallow connections he'd grown so used to. But now, it seemed he was just another secret.

Trying to shake the disappointment, Louis walked back toward the bar, where Karen was waiting, with a smile.

"Shots?" he asked.

"Go for it!" she replied, her smile wide.

With each shot, the world around him blurred. The music, his friends' laughter, and the night's noise merged into a swirling haze. He didn't care anymore, and he didn't want to care.

As the night wore on, the effects of the alcohol started to show. Stumbling slightly, he waved off his friend's concerned looks.

"Are you sure you're all right Louis?" Lauren asked, raising an eyebrow.

"Absolutely!" Louis grinned, slinging an arm around her shoulder. "Let's dance!"

Before he knew it, he pulled Lauren back to the dance floor, twirling in the moment. Everything felt far away—his worries, his doubts—just the rhythm and the freedom to let go.

Hours later, Louis woke to the familiar stuffiness of Sarah's Room. The heat radiating from the heater pulled him from his deep sleep. His head throbbed, and he could not remember how he ended up in her house.

"Morning, Billy Elliot," Karen mumbled, opening one eye. "You went for it last night."

Louis groaned, burying his face in the pillow. "I am fucking sweating – that heating's never off in this house. How did we even get here? I don't even remember leaving Bakers."

"You were a mess! Thought you were going to end up on the bar," Karen laughed, stretching.

Louis sighed, feeling the weight of the night sink in. "Great. A reputation to go with the headache."

"More like a legend," Karen teased. "So, kiss any boys?" she asked with a grin.

Louis hesitated, then quickly masked his feelings. "Who, me? No way! I'm not even gay Karen" he replied with a sly smirk.

Karen laughed. "Nice Joke Louis, you are the campest guy I know! Even Jo knows you are gay!"

Louis laughed confused. "Who's Jo?"

"Jo Mama" Karen replied before bursting into a fit of laughter. "Man Louis, I get you every single time!" she took a deep breath and continued. "Gullible and gay, well my little gay boy I don't know about you, but I think a greasy breakfast is in order."

Louis laughed, grateful to Karen for always being able to make him laugh. "Ha – yeah, I wouldn't mind a sausage to be fair".

The pair dragged themselves out of bed and out of the bedroom they laughed their way into the kitchen, but Louis's thoughts kept drifting back to the events of last night—Paul's kiss, his sudden departure, and the painful words that followed.

He wasn't sure what to do with the mixed emotions inside him. The rush of excitement, the betrayal, the confusion—it all felt too much.

But as Karen chatted away, the normalcy and the comfort of friendship, grounded him. Maybe he didn't have all the answers yet, but at least he knew one thing for sure—he wouldn't let last night spoil everything good in his life.

Someday, he thought, he'd find something tangible without secrets or hidden agendas. For now, though, he was content to enjoy the warmth of the people who had always been there for him.

CHAPTER TWO
CHASING THE TARDIS

A few days after the wild night out, Louis found himself back in his bedroom, the dim glow of a streetlight cast a soft wash over the space. The room was split down the middle: one side held his bed, the other an empty one intended for his younger brother Jamie, who lived with their Dad. The untouched bed symbolized a closeness that Louis longed for—Jamie's laughter, shared games, and the sense of family that felt so rare these days.

Sprawled out on his slightly lumpy mattress, Louis still thought about his recent kiss with Paul. The thrill had been undeniable, but now confusion lingered in his mind. Before he could linger too long, his iPad chimed from the nightstand, pulling him back. He opened it to find an email:

Subject: Exciting Opportunity - Doctor Who Dalek Escape Room

Dear Louis,

I hope this finds you well! I'm reaching out because I recently read your blog piece on Doctor Who and was genuinely impressed. Your passion for the series comes through so clearly, and I think you'd be an excellent fit for an

event we're hosting. We invite you to Reading, London, to review our new Dalek escape room, "A Dalek Awakens." We could also arrange an interview with Nicholas Briggs, the voice of the Daleks. Let me know if you're interested, and we'll discuss the details.

Best,
Clara Thompson
Manager, Escape Hunt UK

Louis's eyes widened, excitement bubbling up as he reread it. Doctor Who had always been his favourite show, and this invitation was an incredible opportunity. Yet, a quick reality check reminded him of the challenge: How will I get to London?

He glanced across at the empty bed, thinking of how his Mum and Gran would feel when he told them. And he couldn't help but wonder what his Dad would think—watching Doctor Who had once been their thing—before they'd drifted apart. Louis could almost hear his Dad's voice explaining plot twists and laughing. The shared bond was like a touchstone of happier times.

Ecstatic, he dashed out of his room, excitement fuelling him as he bounded down the stairs.

"Mum!" he called out, bursting into the living room where she was curled up with Mika, their dog, watching Netflix. Her eyes lit up as she looked over.

35

"What's up?" she asked, her expression turning curious.

"I just got an email—they want me to review a Doctor Who Dalek escape room! And I might get to interview Nicholas Briggs!"

His Mum's face broke into a proud smile. "That's fantastic, Louis! I'm so proud of you!"

"I know!" he said, unable to keep from grinning. "Only... I have to figure out how I'll get to London."

"We'll make it work," she said, reassuring him. "This is such a great chance for you!"

Back in his room, Louis lay sprawled across his bed, staring up at the ceiling. His iPad rested beside him, with the email from Clara still open. A trip to London... the idea filled him with excitement.

He glanced over at his worn old school backpack lying by the door. It held the basics: textbooks, notebooks, and his planner, where he'd carefully pencilled in everything from assignment deadlines to reminders about watching his spending. London hadn't been part of that plan. But something about this felt different—he'd regret it if he missed this chance.

Sitting up, he pulled his iPad closer and replied, accepting Clara's invitation. He then got to work searching for bus fares. A late-night coach was leaving Sunday that would get him into London by Monday morning. His heart pounded as he scrolled through the options, each a reminder of how much of his student loan he'd have to part with to make this happen.

His student loan had come through this month, a sum he'd promised to ration carefully. But what if.. what if this was worth it? He couldn't shake the thought that this wasn't just any opportunity. Interviewing an actor from Doctor Who could open doors, he'd only dreamed of. Wasn't that what he'd taken the loan out for in the first place—to chase his ambitions and set himself up for the future?

With a mix of nerves and excitement, he pressed the button. As he confirmed the payment, a thrill ran through him—a feeling he hadn't had. For once, he was betting on himself.

He sat his iPad down, a grin spreading across his face. London was calling, and he was ready to answer.

Staring at the ceiling, Louis let the rush of excitement from his upcoming trip mix with the quieter memories of his past. The email invitation still glowed on his iPad screen, its words reflecting the opportunity he'd just been offered and a connection to something that had shaped him profoundly. This wasn't just about a trip to London or a meeting with a famous voice actor; it was about the part of him that had once been forged during nights watching Doctor Who beside his Dad.

He glanced over at the empty bed across the room, the one meant for Jamie, and an ache of familiarity settled over him. Memories of family Saturday nights flickered back like old snapshots: Dad's easy laughter, the smell of popcorn, the sense of security he felt knowing he had someone to share those adventures with. It all felt close yet impossibly far away, a bond that had faded over time.

His eyes fell on the dormant TV hanging on his bedroom wall; he was three years old again, fresh from a bath, a towel wrapped around him as his Dad whisked him into his favourite blue pyjamas. His Dad's laughter echoed in his ears as he hurried him onto the couch, just in time for the start of the very first episode of the Doctor Who reboot.

He remembered the warmth of his Dad's arm around him, the way his small body fit perfectly in the crook of his Dad's side. The music had begun, and the thrill of the TARDIS rushing through the stars had pulled him in. He had felt like he was transported to another world with his Dad beside him, explaining every twist and turn, sharing that sense of wonder.

His Dad had been his guide to the mysteries of the universe on-screen and off, gently explaining the Doctor's quirks, laughing at his oddities, and bringing Louis along on that journey. And even as he grew older, their Saturday nights remained special, a bridge between them that felt unbreakable.

But that was before the separation. Louis had kept up the tradition, but he watched Doctor Who alone these days, replaying old episodes in the quiet of his room or tuning into the latest series.

Every time the familiar logo flashed on the screen, he felt a bittersweet sting—a reminder of what he and his Dad had once shared and what felt missing now.

Louis drew his knees up to his chest, wrapping his arms around them as he stared at the TV, its dark screen reflecting his face. He could still see the little boy he used to be, waiting eagerly for the next adventure with his Dad. The tradition might have faded, but the memories remained vivid, clinging to him like an old song that still made his heart skip a beat.

With a quiet sigh, he picked up the remote and turned on the TV. The familiar Doctor Who logo flashed on the screen, and for a few hours, he let himself be that little boy again, waiting for the magic to unfold. In all its wonder, the show was still there for him—something that connected him to his past and the dreams that now lay ahead.

The next day didn't feel like any Thursday for Louis. Walking onto campus, he felt a thrill sparking in his veins, the morning sun shone through the campus buildings as if illuminating the path ahead just for him. In class, he spotted Megan in her seat, her notebook open.

"Hey, Megan!" he called, heading over.

"Hey! What's up?" she replied, her eyes lighting up with curiosity.

"I have some big news!" Louis leaned in, lowering his voice. "I'm going to London to review a new Dalek escape room and interview Nicholas Briggs—the voice of the Daleks!"

Megan's eyes widened in surprise. "No way! That's incredible! Doctor Who is your favourite, right?"

"Yeah! It's a dream come true." He grinned, feeling a rush of joy at her reaction.

Megan beamed, sharing his excitement. "You've got to take loads of pictures for your blog! When do you leave?"

"On Monday. I just got the email yesterday," Louis explained, still buzzing from the news.

Just then, his phone vibrated. He pulled it out, seeing a call from his Gran. "Hang on," he said to Megan before answering. "Gran! Guess what—I'm going to London!"

"I just heard from your Mum!" she exclaimed, her voice brimming with pride. "I'm so happy for you! This is amazing, Louis. Take plenty of pictures—I want to see everything!"

"I will, Gran," he promised, smiling.

When he hung up, he turned back to Megan, who was still beaming. "I've told everyone—my Mum, Gran, a few friends—but I haven't told my Dad yet."

"Why not?" Megan asked, her eyes softening.

Louis sighed, the excitement fading slightly. "I'm worried he might not pick up. It's complicated with us."

40

Megan nodded, understanding. "It makes sense. I hope he'll listen when you tell him, though. Maybe this news could bring you closer."

Louis settled into his seat as the lecturer entered, trying to focus, but his thoughts drifted. Sharing this news with his Dad felt daunting, yet he couldn't shake the hope it might bridge the distance between them.

After college, Louis spotted Sarah sitting on the steps, scrolling on her phone. She looked up as he approached.

"There he is—the soon-to-be-famous Doctor Who journalist!" she teased, standing to greet him.

Louis laughed, rolling his eyes. "You make it sound like I'm going to be a celebrity."

"Hey, this is huge!" she said, linking her arm with his as they walked to the bus stop. "An escape room review and an interview with Nicholas Briggs! You're practically on your way to the red carpet."

On the bus, they took their usual seats at the back, where they could talk uninterrupted. Louis shared all the details, her enthusiasm fuelling his excitement.

When the bus finally pulled up to Sarah's stop, she stood, gathering her things. "You're still coming out on Saturday. Saturday nights in town are our new thing! '

Louis chuckled, shifting in his seat. "I don't know. I've got the bus to London on Sunday night—I should probably be responsible."

She rolled her eyes, laughing. "As if that's ever stopped you! Come on, Louis. Just for a bit?"

He pretended to consider, but she grinned, sensing she'd won. "All right, all right. Text me the plan."

"Perfect! Also, there's something I've been meaning to tell you," Sarah began, pausing thoughtfully.

Louis looked over, sensing her excitement. "Yeah? What's up?"

"I met someone," she said, her blush deepening. "We've been on a few dates, and he's nice. I mean, like, genuinely nice." She laughed a little, looking slightly embarrassed. "His name's Paul."

The name hit Louis like a shockwave, bringing back flashes of that night at the club—Paul's charm, unexpected kiss, distant exit, and strange insistence on keeping things quiet because of Sarah. Louis held his expression steady, hiding the rush of mixed emotions, and nodded as she spoke.

"That's great, Sarah," he said, smiling warmly. "I'm happy for you."

"Thanks, Louis. I didn't want to say anything until I was sure, but... yeah. He's sweet, and he makes me laugh," she said, her eyes shining with happiness. "It's early, but I think I might like him."

Louis felt a knot in his chest, a conflict he couldn't fully name. She looked genuinely happy, and he couldn't bring up what had happened with Paul. She deserved this moment of joy, uncomplicated.

"Honestly, that's amazing," he replied, nudging her gently. "You deserve someone like that."

The bus halted to a stop, and Sarah smiled at him as she stepped off the bus and walked towards her street.

That night, Louis lay in bed with Mika, freshly bathed and cosy in his pyjamas, watching Doctor Who. Just as the Doctor's voice filled the room, a soft knock sounded on his door. He paused the episode as his Mum entered, holding a cup of coffee, her expression uncharacteristically sombre.

"Hey, Mum," he greeted, but the sight of her sad smile made his fade.

She walked over slowly, sitting down at the end of his bed. She stared at the empty bed across the room momentarily, her eyes glistening in the low light. "You know how much I love you, Louis," she began softly, her voice catching. "And how proud I am of you… of everything you're doing."

Louis sat up, sensing something more profound in her words. "I know, Mum. I couldn't have done it without you."

She smiled at that, then looked away as if searching for words. "We've been through a lot together, haven't we? From… from when you were little, through everything with your Dad and the divorce." Her voice trembled, and she held her coffee tightly, gazing at Jamie's empty bed beside him.

"You're getting a lot of what I wanted to give you both," she murmured, a tear slipping down her cheek. "Sometimes, I just wish… I could do the same for Jamie."

Louis's heart ached to see her this way, the weight of years and sacrifices clear in her expression. "Mum, you've always been the best. You were always there for me, reading my stories and ensuring I felt loved. And you'll be able to do that one day with Jamie, too—he's got so much to look forward to with you."

She nodded, but her sadness lingered as she leaned in, pulling him close. The warmth of her hug brought him back to his childhood, and he felt the strength and comfort that only his Mum could provide.

She kissed him softly on the forehead, brushing his hair back. "Promise me you'll do well in life, Louis. Promise you won't… end up like me?"

Louis looked at her, confusion flickering in his eyes. "What do you mean, Mum? You're amazing."

A faint, bittersweet smile tugged at her lips. "I threw away my dreams once. I wanted to be the best Mum I could be for you and your brothers, to be there no matter what it took. But… It's hard sometimes, and I feel like I lost a part of myself along the way. Some days, my mind feels like a storm I can't escape."

She paused, taking a deep breath, her eyes darkening with emotion. "But I want more for you. I want you to be stronger than I could be… to have dreams you don't let go of."

Louis's heart ached, seeing her bear the struggles she carried alone. "You've done so much for us, Mum," he whispered, his voice thick. "And I'll work hard—I'll make you proud."

She reached over, stroking his cheek one last time before standing up. "I know you will, sweetheart." She lingered in the doorway, giving him one last, loving look. "Goodnight, Louis. Sleep well."

"Goodnight, Mum," he replied softly, watching her leave.

As the door closed, Louis remained still, the soft click echoing in the quiet room. His Mum's words hung like a song long after the final note. She'd weathered so many storms alone; sacrifices he was only beginning to understand.

He looked around his room—the faded posters, the well-worn bedspread, Jamie's untouched bed standing across from his own like a silent reminder of family ties stretched thin. His mind replayed the times his Mum had been his shield and sanctuary, steady even when life weighed her down. A pang of pride and sorrow rose in him, twining together in a way he couldn't entirely untangle.

Lying back down, he pulled his blanket up to his chin, staring at the ceiling as his thoughts raced. The dreams he held onto suddenly felt sharper, brighter, like stars just within reach. This Doctor Who opportunity felt like the start of something bigger. But as excitement bubbled up, so did a quiet, unspoken promise. He wouldn't let her sacrifices go unnoticed. He wouldn't let his dreams slip through his fingers.

"Thanks, Mum," he whispered as if she could still hear him through the walls. In the gentle quiet, he let his eyes close, the thrill of possibility mingling with the warmth of her love. He drifted into sleep, ready for whatever came next.

Louis awoke the next morning to a soft knock on his door, followed by his Mum's voice calling through. "Morning, love. I was thinking of heading to Gran's today; would you like to come along?"

He blinked, the idea of seeing Gran pulling him entirely from his sleep. It had been a few weeks since his last visit, and the thought of her warm smile and cosy house was just what he needed. "Yeah, definitely," he said, stretching as he sat up. Gran's house was a sanctuary where everything felt simpler, and he could forget about the pressures of the outside world, even if just for a day.

Downstairs, his Mum was already pulling on her coat. Mika's tail wagged in excitement, nosing at the leash in his Mum's hand, eager for the trip.

The bus ride through the countryside was peaceful, and Louis watched the passing landscape with a sense of nostalgia. His mind wandered to the months he'd spent living with Gran during the separation. Her house had always felt like a refuge— familiar, full of comforting scents and quiet corners where he could be himself. The lavender lingered in each room, the warmth of the fire crackling in the living room and the ever-colourful garden that had always felt alive, even in the chill of early spring.

When they arrived, Gran's dogs, Bonnie and Bella—sisters with matching black-and-white coats—came bounding to the door, barking in greeting. Gran appeared soon after, her face lighting up with a smile that always made Louis feel welcome.

"There you are, my darling!" she called, pulling him into a hug that felt like coming home.

The house was exactly as he remembered: oak floors gleaming softly in the afternoon light, family photos on the walls, and the comfortable clutter of well-loved knick-knacks. They settled into the living room, where Gran had already laid out tea and biscuits, and Louis relaxed, letting the comforting atmosphere wash over him.

As he sipped his tea, his gaze fell on the sofa where he had come out as gay to his family, his hand resting in Gran's as she reassured him with words still echoing in his heart. That night had been one of acceptance and love, a turning point in his life. Gran had told him she was proud of him, and her support had been unwavering.

"I've missed this place," he murmured, glancing around the room, Bonnie and Bella nestled beside him. "It feels like coming home."

Gran's smile softened as she took his hand. "You'll always have a home here, Louis. I hope you know that."

Louis nodded; his chest full of gratitude. "I do, Gran. I do."

They spent the afternoon catching up. Gran listened sparklingly as Louis recounted the details of his upcoming Doctor Who adventure, the escape room, and his interview with Nicholas Briggs. Her pride was clear, and she asked thoughtful questions, always encouraging him to pursue his dreams.

Later, as the fire crackled softly, Louis remembered the special Christmas morning he'd spent with Gran. They had sat beside the fire, unwrapping presents just the two of them, and she had given him a Doctor Who mug and a scarf she'd knitted herself. Her gentle laugh had filled the room, and she had taken his hand, telling him that no matter what life threw his way, he would always have people who loved him.

The memory wrapped around him like a warm blanket, and he smiled as he watched the flames dance in the hearth. Those quiet memories of support and love had shaped him more than he realized.

That night, Louis lay in his old bedroom, the familiar quilt draped over him. Despite the world changing around him, here, he felt calm. He knew that no matter what happened, he would always have a place to return to, a place of unconditional love.

The following morning, the scent of Gran's breakfast filled the house—toast and poached eggs, his favourite. Louis shuffled into the kitchen, the warmth of the room greeting him. Gran stood at the stove, expertly flipping the toast while watching the eggs. The table was set with two plates, and the comforting routine of their mornings together felt like a balm to Louis's soul.

"Morning, love! Come and get it!" Gran called; her voice filled with cheer.

He took a seat, savouring the aroma. "Wow, this smells amazing."

"Only the best for my favourite grandson," she teased, her eyes twinkling.

As they ate, the television flickered on in the background. The news anchor's voice cut through the room, talking about the rising number of COVID-19 cases and government warnings. Louis's stomach dropped slightly at the sound of those words, significantly when Gran paused mid-bite, concern crossing her face.

"Louis, have you been keeping up with this? It sounds like things are getting serious."

"Yeah," he replied, trying to keep his voice steady. "I saw some updates. They're saying there are more cases in London, and it's spreading fast."

Gran's brow furrowed. "You're heading down there tomorrow night for that Doctor Who thing. Do you think it's safe?"

The excitement that had once filled him now mixed with a tinge of anxiety. "I don't know, Gran. It feels like such a big opportunity, but... it's scary, too."

Gran reached across the table, taking his hand. "You must be careful, love. But if you want this, maybe you should take the risk."

He looked up, surprised by her encouragement. "Are you sure?"

"Of course! But be smart about it. Wear a mask, use hand sanitiser, and keep your distance as much as possible. Just don't put yourself at unnecessary risk," she advised, her voice steady.

"I will, I promise," he said, a mix of relief and apprehension settling in. Gran's words comforted him, but he knew there were risks.

Gran smiled warmly. "No opportunity is worth your health, but if you feel it's worth pursuing, I support you."

As they continued to watch the news, the updates became more alarming. Louis couldn't shake the unease that had settled in his chest.

"I can't believe how quickly everything is changing," he muttered, his mind swirling. "What if I get there and it all falls apart?"

Gran squeezed his hand, her grip solid. "Whatever happens, you always have a home here with me. We'll figure it out together. You're not alone."

Her words brought him some peace. He felt grateful for her unwavering support and the warmth of the house around him, even as the world outside seemed to shift.

They finished breakfast, the news growing more alarming in the background. Afterwards, Gran suggested they spend some time in the garden before he had to leave. Louis's spirits lifted at the thought of working with the plants in the sunny garden, a peaceful escape.

"Sounds perfect," he said, his mind distracted from his worries.

Sarah had mentioned Saturday nights were their new night for meeting in town for drinks, so he would need to leave soon, but he was excited for this time to be outside, working alongside Gran.

Just then, his Mum appeared from the bathroom, towel wrapped around her hair. "Morning! Did I miss breakfast?"

"Not at all!" Louis replied, gesturing for her to join them. "Gran made my favourite."

She smiled, moving to the table. "Thanks, Mum." She turned to Gran. "Thank you for always taking care of us."

Gran's smile was soft, and the moment's warmth filled the room as they settled back into their routine.

"So, are you feeling okay about London tomorrow?" his mother asked, her brow furrowed with concern.

"I think so," Louis replied, trying to sound confident. "I'll be careful."

His Mum nodded, her worry still visible. "Remember, wear your mask, keep your distance, and don't hesitate to turn back if it feels too risky."

"I will, I will," he assured her, feeling the weight of their concern and the love that came with it.

Louis knelt in Gran's Garden, the sun casting a warm glow over the vibrant flowers. Gran carefully pruned the roses while Louis worked on the vegetable patch. Mika, Bonnie, and Bella were nearby, playing in the garden, their laughter and energy filling the air.

"You've got your hands full with those three!" Louis teased, watching his Mum tumble onto the grass after Mika.

"Just trying to tire them out before lunch!" she laughed.

Louis soaked in the joy around him soothing his nerves. But as the time passed, he glanced at the clock. "Hey, Gran, I should head back home soon. I've got to get ready for tonight with my friends."

"Oh, that's right! Just a few drinks?" Gran asked.

"Yeah," Louis replied, a mix of nerves and excitement in his voice. "And I need to pack for tomorrow."

"Just be careful," his Mum called, finally getting Mika to sit.

"I will," Louis assured them, feeling the weight of the situation and the love surrounding him.

Gran nodded; her eyes soft. "Take care of yourself, Louis. We want you to have fun, but your safety comes first."

Louis bent to give Bonnie a scratch behind the ears before straightening. "Thanks for today, Gran. It's been nice working outside."

"You're always welcome in my garden," Gran said, her eyes twinkling as he waved goodbye.

With one last glance at his Mum and a quick pat for Mika, Louis headed home. The garden's warmth and his family's support stayed with him even as he prepared for the uncertainties ahead.

CHAPTER THREE
DANCING WITH UNCERTAINTY

As Louis stepped through the front door, the familiar scent of his home wrapped around him. The house was too quiet, and it felt like the stillness was pressing on him. He hadn't expected the loneliness to hit so hard after the warmth of the evening with his Mum and Gran. The contrast was sharp, but he shrugged it off, sighing and hanging up his coat.

His phone buzzed on the counter, pulling him from his thoughts. He glanced at the message from Sarah, and a wave of anticipation bubbled up in his chest. It read:

Hey! I can't wait for tonight! Are you still good for First Ed?

He typed back quickly:

Absolutely! Will see you there!

A grin spread across his face. He felt the excitement begin to trickle in, his earlier unease starting to slip away. The thought of another Saturday surrounded by his friend's energy was precisely what he needed. He turned toward the bathroom, determined to unwind before heading out.

He turned on the tap, he let the hot water fill the bathtub, the sound soothing against the quiet of the empty house. As the water rose, he pulled out a bright bath bomb from his Lush collection—his favourite, a calming lavender and chamomile blend. He dropped it in, watching it fizz and swirl, the scent filling the room, grounding him in the peaceful moment.

As he sank into the water, his mind drifted back to Gran's Garden earlier that day. The sun had been warm on his face, the birds were singing, and everything had felt right. That feeling— of clarity, of peace—was something he wanted to carry with him.

After bathing, Louis dressed in his favourite NICCE jumper and jeans that fit just right. He ran a quick hand through his hair, checking his reflection with a casual smile before grabbing his trusty, well-worn backpack from behind the door. It had been with him through many adventures, and he was about to add another one. He packed a few essentials for his trip to London—his toothbrush, some toiletries, his charger, and a couple of notebooks for jotting down ideas. The act of preparing, of getting ready, grounded him. It was a small thing, but it helped.

Once his bag was packed and ready to go for tomorrow, he called a taxi to take him to First Edition. He felt the anticipation rise again and the nervous flutter of knowing that tomorrow would be immense. Gran's words from breakfast echoed in his head: *"You'll always have a home here with me."* It was a comforting thought, one that kept his resolve steady. No matter what happened his future never went to plan- he had people who cared about him.

When the taxi pulled up outside, Louis took a deep breath and stepped into the cool night air, his thoughts lost to the quiet hum of his hometown. The ride to First Edition was short; and soon enough, the liveliness of the busy town enveloped him. He spotted Sarah standing outside, her grin widening when she saw him.

"Oi! There he is!" she called, waving.

Louis couldn't help but grin back. "Hey! I'm so excited for London tomorrow," he said, his nerves quickly replaced by the comfort of her easy energy.

They greeted each other with a hug, and Sarah turned to him with a mischievous grin. "You're going to love it. I can see you geeking out over everything."

They headed inside to meet the others—Karen, Lauren, and Carly—already gathered by the bar. They welcomed Louis with hugs, and Sarah ordered a round of shots without hesitation.

"To tomorrow night," she said, raising her glass.

"To Louis, the Whovian," Karen added, and they all clinked glasses, throwing back the shots in one swift motion. Louis felt the warmth of the alcohol spread through him, the initial nerves giving way to a sense of lightness.

The DJ started playing "Dancing Queen," and the girls squealed, immediately pulling Louis onto the dance floor. The music washed over him, filling the space between them with pure energy. Louis laughed, his earlier doubts forgotten as they twirled and sang along to the song.

"Abba just gets it!" Carly shouted, spinning Louis around. The carefree atmosphere was infectious, and he felt completely lost in the moment.

The night stretched on, and Louis and Sarah found themselves outside in the smoking area. The soft glow of the string lights made the air feel dreamlike, but Louis couldn't shake the gnawing feeling of something unresolved. He took a drag from the cigarette that Sarah had given him, wincing slightly as the smoke stung his throat.

He was trying to let go, to immerse himself in the night, but the thought of his Dad once again lingered in the back of his mind. He had hoped his father would at least call before the trip and share in Louis' excitement. Did his Dad know? Had anyone told him?

Suddenly, Sarah's voice cut through his thoughts. "Oh my God, there's Paul! I didn't think I would see him tonight—he was at the football," she said before excusing herself. "I'll be right back, okay?" She handed him her pack of cigarettes and rushed away.

Louis's heart sank as she left, his mind at once jumping to the thought of Paul—the same Paul he'd once been texting, the one who had shared a kiss with him—the one who had made everything feel so complicated.

He tried to shake off the feeling. He needed a distraction. Reaching for his phone, he dialled his Dad's number, eager to tell him about tomorrow's plans.

The call rang once, then twice, before going to voicemail. He waited, staring at the screen, wishing for a voice on the other end. Maybe a word of encouragement for the trip. But the silence that followed only made him feel more distant, more disconnected.

He stood there, the weight of his phone in his hand a reminder of what was missing. His Dad's absence felt heavier now, even though he had been trying to move past it.

With a sigh, Louis slipped his phone back into his pocket and crushed his cigarette. He wasn't sure if it was the loneliness or just the night's high, but he needed to take his mind off things. He turned back toward the bar, where the music still thumped through the walls, the familiar chaos beckoning him.

Inside, Karen pulled him aside, holding out a small clear bag. "I've got some pills. Want in?"

Louis froze. His mind raced. He knew it wasn't a good idea, but the weight of the night—the pressure, the confusion, the emptiness—made him waver. He could feel the pull of the crowd, the sense of belonging that might come from just letting go.

Through a window, he could see Sarah and Paul, still in the smoking area, laughing, their carefree energy seeping into the air. Louis could almost hear their joy from where he stood, and his ache deepened. Maybe just for a few hours, he could be like them, be happy— and forget everything else.

But before he could stop himself, he nodded. "Yeah, why not?"

The pill was small, but it felt heavy as he accepted it. It took hold gradually, a warmth unfurling from his core and spreading like a soft wave through his limbs. As the music thumped around him, Louis felt his heartbeat sync with the bass, each beat vibrating through his body, filling him with an electrifying energy he could not quite explain.

His senses were heightened—every light seemed to pulse, colours blurred into one another, and the heat on the dance floor wrapped around him like a heavy blanket. His friends' faces were a swirl of grins and glittering eyes, all amplified by the rhythm driving them together.

But the intensity came with its edges. His jaw began to ache from grinding his teeth unconsciously, the tightness creeping into his temples, a dull ache beneath the rush. His skin felt damp, beads of sweat tracing his forehead and neck, but he hardly noticed, lost in the pounding beat and flashing lights. It was like the whole room was a single, pulsating entity, each person moving in sync, caught up in the same unrelenting rhythm.

He felt alive, euphoric, and untethered, but somewhere in the back of his mind, he sensed a tension, like a string pulled just a bit too tight.

As the hours ticked on, he hadn't even noticed Sarah's return. The night spun into a kaleidoscope of laughter, music, and neon light flashes. Everything blurred—faces, drinks, the relentless beat of the music pulsing through his veins. Time lost its meaning, folding in on itself as Louis floated from one song to the following, one conversation to another, Sarah and the others at his side, all of them swept up in the dizzying current.

When the early hours rolled around, Louis stumbled outside, the cool air hitting him like a slap to the face. The weight of his backpack at home, packed for tomorrow's trip, was a reminder of what was supposed to be a new chapter. But now, after everything, he wasn't sure what he was stepping into anymore.

The streets were eerily quiet as he made his way home. The night's excitement had faded, leaving behind a calm, hollow feeling. Tomorrow was waiting, but Louis wasn't sure what to expect. What had seemed so clear earlier now felt like another step into the unknown.

Louis jolted awake. Rubbing his eyes, he squinted at his phone screen—5:00 p.m. Panic hit him. He had missed the bus that was supposed to get him to Glasgow in time for his night bus to London. *Sunday service.* He groaned in frustration- The buses only ran every hour.

His head throbbed, his throat parched and raw. When he spoke, his voice was hoarse, and the pounding in his temples felt like a cruel reminder of last night's chaos. His room seemed to spin slightly, but he forced himself upright, stumbling to the bathroom to shake off the lingering fog of sleep and alcohol.

The bath's hot water stung initially, but he settled in, letting the steam ease his sore muscles. The fog in his mind slowly began to lift, leaving him more awake, yet drained. By the time he had scrubbed off the remnants of the night before and changed into fresh clothes, he felt slightly more human. But the anxiety was

60

still gnawing at him. He had to figure out how to get to Glasgow fast.

Downstairs, his Mum was in the kitchen, Mika curled up by her feet, sipping coffee and watching the clock. She glanced at Louis as he entered, the concern in her eyes quickly shifting to resignation. She knew the drill.

"I know, I know," Louis mumbled, rubbing his sore head. "I messed up... overslept. Last night just... got out of hand."

"Well, maybe this is a good lesson in not going all out the night before something important," she said with a gentle smile, nudging a notepad toward him. "Write down my number, and Gran's too. Just in case. London's not close, and you might need it if your phone dies."

Louis took the pen, scrawling the numbers onto the notepad, his Mum watching with that look he knew all too well— love mixed with a bit of worry. He tore out the page and put it into his pocket. When he'd finished, he lingered by the table before returning upstairs. The anxiety still prickled at him, but he felt a strange comfort from her practicality, a steady anchor that grounded him a bit.

Louis grabbed his backpack from where he'd left it on the bed, feeling its familiar weight settle against his shoulders. It was scuffed and worn but had been with him through countless trips and adventures. With a quick check, he confirmed everything was still inside—his charger, AirPods, his outfit, and his small collection of toiletries. Satisfied, he slung it over one shoulder,

61

the contents feeling like a reassuring bundle of everything he'd need for the journey.

Before he left his room, he knelt beside his bed, pulling out an old shoebox he hadn't touched in ages. Inside were memories, keepsakes he'd saved over the years. As he sifted through them, his hand brushed against two small LEGO figures he'd built back in the Glasgow LEGO store—a tiny version of himself and one he'd made to look like his Mum, with a bright smile and brown LEGO hair.

He tucked the figure of his Mum into his pocket and grabbed the miniature figure of himself. As he headed downstairs and into the kitchen, he held it out to his Mum.

"I know it's silly, but... here. You can hold onto this if you miss me while I'm gone."

Her expression softened, and she smiled and took the tiny figure from him.

"I'll carry yours with me, too," Louis added, tapping his pocket. "That way, I'll have you with me, even if it's just LEGO you."

She chuckled, shaking her head affectionately. "You're a soft one, Lou, but I wouldn't have it any other way."

Louis rechecked the time, the panic bubbling up. "God, I'm going to have to book a taxi to Glasgow. I've missed the bus and can't wait for the next one."

His Mum nodded, ruffling his hair fondly. "Just make sure you get there, all right? And keep your phone charged."

He hugged her goodbye, feeling the reassuring weight of his backpack against her arm. With one last kiss for Mika, Louis stepped outside, the cool air of the evening a jarring contrast to the warmth inside. He took a deep breath, mentally preparing for the chaos of the journey ahead.

As Louis rounded the corner of the house, he checked over his shoulder to ensure his Mum wasn't watching. The pack of menthol cigarettes Sarah had handed him the night before was tucked into his pocket. He pulled one out, the crackle of the lighter illuminating his face. The smoke cut through the fog of his hangover, soothing his throat and nerves. He inhaled deeply, feeling the anxiety settle as the cigarette calmed him.

He watched the smoke trail upwards; each drag grounding him a little more, the panic ebbing just enough for him to think straight. The sound of a car engine in the distance caught his attention, and he quickly flicked the cigarette away, slipping the packet back into his pocket, before heading back to the front of the house.

The taxi arrived, the middle-aged driver offering a friendly smile as Louis climbed in.

"Where to, son?" the driver asked, adjusting his rearview mirror.

"Buchanan Bus Station," Louis replied, already scanning the route in his mind. "I've got a bus to London tonight."

The driver nodded and began conversing as they pulled away from his house. Louis explained his reason for the trip—an interview with Nicholas Briggs from Doctor Who—and his hopes to break into journalism eventually.

"Good for you! That's a tough field, but if you're passionate, you'll do well," the driver said with a chuckle, a note of encouragement.

Louis grinned, feeling a tiny spark of excitement. He continued, talking about his love for storytelling and helping people feel heard through his writing. The driver nodded knowingly.

"Yeah, we need more of that. Hopefully, you'll have plenty of stories of your own to tell," the driver added as they passed through the streets of Glasgow.

When they reached Buchanan Bus Station, Louis paid the driver, thanked him, and stepped out into the bustle of travellers. With thirty minutes to spare before his bus, his stomach rumbled. He spotted a KFC nearby—perfect.

Inside, he ordered a box meal and found a seat. He munched on fries and sipped his drink while people-watching. He saw the other passengers chatting; some were lost in their own worlds. The food did its job, dulling the worst of his hangover.

Upon finishing his meal, he returned to the bus station, the weight of his backpack on his shoulder comforting him again. He checked his phone, confirming that his bus departed from Stance three.

When the bus pulled in, its headlights cut through the dark evening, Louis joined the line of passengers and boarded. He

walked down the aisle, scanning the seats for his preferred spot—
the back. It felt familiar, comforting in its distance from everyone
else. He liked the anonymity, the quiet space.

Settling in, he plugged his phone into the USB slot and
queued up his playlist, choosing "The Man" from Taylor Swift's
new album 'Lover'. The song's rhythm matched the humming of
the bus as they drove out of the station.

He watched the scenery change as they drove out of the
city, the bright lights of Glasgow slowly fading as they hit the
dark motorway. The bus was headed to Edinburgh first, a short
stop to pick up more travellers before the longer stretch to
London. The rhythm of the road, the hum of the engine, and
Swift's voice created a cocoon around him. It felt almost
surreal—him, off to London on a whim, a chance to leave behind
his familiar routines for a day, and maybe, just maybe, figure out
something new about himself along the way. As they rolled into
Edinburgh, Louis glanced out the window, catching a view of the
castle illuminated against the midnight sky. Its ancient stones
glowed softly in the darkness, towering above the quiet, watching
over Edinburgh's slumber. The streets were nearly empty, the city
wrapped in an almost mystical calm that made his journey feel
more momentous.

The bus eased into Edinburgh's bus station, hissing to a
stop. A few more passengers boarded, shifting through the rows
until a woman—a short, middle-aged redhead with a mess of
curls, wearing a green jacket and carrying a purple shoulder

bag—made her way down the aisle. Louis watched her approach, realizing his only available seat was beside him. She smiled briefly, a bit sheepishly, before settling into the seat beside him.

CHAPTER FOUR
REFLECTIONS ON THE ROAD

After the bus left Edinburgh, Louis had fallen asleep with his head resting against the window. As he stirred from his nap, the bus rolling along the road almost lulled him back to sleep. The soft hum of the engine was a comforting rhythm, but the dull ache of his hangover still seemed to press against his skull. He blinked and rubbed his eyes, the soft blue light from the bus interior helping him focus.

The woman next to him, the one with the green jacket and bright red curls, had been silent for a while now, her face buried in her phone as the landscape outside shifted from darkened streets to the open motorway. Louis glanced over at her, noticing how at ease she looked despite the journey's late hour. He envied her calm—something he hadn't felt in a few days.

She noticed him staring and raised an eyebrow, offering a small smile. "You look like you could use some help," she said, her voice smooth and warm, carrying an accent that was neither entirely British nor foreign. Louis couldn't place it.

"Yeah, that's probably true," he muttered, running a hand through his messy hair. "Long trip."

She nodded in understanding. "I'm Helga, by the way."

He returned her smile with a tired one of his own. "Louis."

"Are you sure you're all right?" she asked, her eyes narrowing slightly as she looked at him with an unexpected kindness, almost as though she could sense his weariness beyond the surface.

Louis hesitated, then shrugged. "Yeah, just... a bit of a rough night last night."

Helga's smile widened. "I get that. It happens to the best of us." She reached into the pocket of her green jacket and pulled out a vape, offering it to him. "Might help take the edge off. If you're not too picky about how you deal with hangovers."

Louis looked at it, then took it from her with a grin. "You're not worried I'll get us both in trouble?"

"Nah," she said with a wink, "you're not the first to need a little distraction on these trips."

Louis took a tentative inhale, the fruity vapour filling his lungs and briefly numbing the edges of his headache. He leaned down, discreetly blowing the vapour beneath the seats. The buzz from it was almost instant, and his shoulders relaxed as he passed the vape back to her.

"Not bad," he said, feeling a bit lighter. Helga tucked the vape back into her pocket, her grin matching his.

"You're welcome," she said softly, her gaze moving to the window. "It's a long ride. Can't hurt to make it that bit more bearable."

Louis lay back in his seat, the vapour still hanging in his chest. He felt the journey would take longer than he expected, but for now, he was okay with it. Even if brief, the quiet camaraderie with Helga helped him push aside the nagging thoughts clawing at him ever since the night before.

The road stretched out before them as the night deepened. Louis let his eyes drift shut, the engine's hum rocking him into a deep, distracted state. His thoughts returned, unbidden, to last night.

It had been a whirlwind. The night's chaos, the drinks, the fleeting conversations, the rush of excitement, and the sudden crash that followed. He'd been looking for something, maybe even trying to escape something, but all he'd found was a reminder of what he didn't have.

The way Paul and Sarah had seemed so effortlessly happy, so connected, while he... hadn't. He felt an ache in his chest, a loneliness he couldn't shake. It had only deepened when he had tried reaching out to his Dad, there had been nothing but silence on the other end.

Louis couldn't help but think how different his life would be if things were easier. If people like Paul and Sarah were more of what he had and less of what he didn't. His fingers drummed restlessly on the seat in front of him.

Helga's voice pulled him from his thoughts. "You sure you're all right?" she asked, her eyes soft and concerned, as if she could sense the shift in his mood.

69

"Yeah," he said quickly, blinking to clear the haze from his mind. "Just... thinking about stuff."

She nodded knowingly, her expression softening. "I get that. Long trips have a way of making you think about everything."

"Yeah..." Louis said, glancing at her again. "You ever feel like... you're just stuck? You're looking for something but can't figure out what it is?"

Helga tilted her head, her lips curling into a small, understanding smile. "All the time. But maybe that's the point— maybe we're not meant to have it all figured out. Sometimes, it's the journey, not the destination."

He thought about that for a few seconds. The journey. He had been so focused on this trip to London—the things he was hoping to do, the purpose he was looking for—that he'd forgotten what he was supposed to be learning along the way.

"Yeah," Louis said quietly, the weight of his thoughts shifting slightly. "I guess you're right."

The bus rolled through the night, and the landscape outside continued to blur into one long stretch of motorway. Louis's mind began to wander, no longer focused on the uncertainty gnawing at him. The quiet of the bus and the company of this stranger, Helga, seemed to provide a brief respite from the noise in his head. Maybe the trip to London wasn't just about meeting

Nicholas Briggs. Perhaps it was about something else he wouldn't fully understand until he reached the journey's end.

For now, though, he was content to let the road unfold before him, the constant hum of the bus, and the steady rhythm of his breath, keeping the edge of the anxiety at bay.

In the end, maybe it was enough to keep going.

Louis felt a gentle nudge on his shoulder, pulling him from the half-daze he'd slipped into while watching the dark landscape blur outside. He glanced over, pulled out his AirPods, and saw the woman beside him offering him a can of Diet Coke.

"Here," she said with a small smile. "Part of my meal deal, but I can't stand the stuff."

"Thanks," he replied, taking it gratefully. "I was so caught up in getting here that I didn't even think to bring snacks. Rookie mistake, I know."

They chatted for a while, sharing the reasons for their journeys. Louis explained his exciting opportunity to interview Nicholas Briggs and review the new escape room. Helga explained how she was visiting her daughter—who had just moved into her new house—for the day.

He checked his phone—5 a.m. Still, a few hours to go. The early morning sky outside was beginning to lighten, soft blues and pinks hinting at dawn. He stifled a yawn, rubbing his eyes, debating whether to get a little more sleep.

"You should try to rest up," Helga suggested, noticing his bleary look. She pulled a small, worn travel pillow from her bag and offered it to him. "It's nothing fancy, but it's saved my neck a few times."

"Thanks, Helga," he said, taking the pillow with a grateful nod. He adjusted it behind his head, settling in with a sigh, closing his eyes, hoping to get a couple more hours before they arrived in the city.

Louis blinked awake and the soft light of dawn began to spill over tall city buildings, casting a warm glow across the bus. Helga smiled beside him.

"We just passed the outskirts of London," she said softly, nodding toward the window. "Thirty more minutes till we're at Victoria."

He turned, his breath catching as he saw the city stretching before him. Commuters hurried along the pavements, cars, and buses weaved through the maze of streets. It felt vast, the buildings towering above, their windows catching the first rays of morning light.

He pressed his forehead to the cool glass, eyes wide with awe. It was nothing like Glasgow. The scale of it, the energy—it was overwhelming. But in an enjoyable way. He'd made it to London.

As the bus wound through the city, nearing Victoria Coach Station, Louis turned to Helga, curiosity laced with a hint of relief in his voice. "So, when are you heading back?"

"I'm on the 10 p.m. bus back to Glasgow tonight," she replied, adjusting her purple bag.

"No way! I'm on that one, too!" Louis grinned. "Guess we're travel buddies till the very end."

They shared a laugh, exchanged Facebook details, and planned to meet in Victoria after their separate adventures. Maybe even go for a drink to catch up.

"Can't wait to hear how it goes," she said warmly.

"Me neither," Louis replied, feeling a little lighter as the bus finally approached the station.

When the bus pulled into Victoria Coach Station, the brakes screeched as it came to a slow stop. Louis and Helga gathered their things, waiting for the crowd to disembark. Once they stepped onto the platform, the sounds of the city—the distant traffic, footsteps, voices blending—filled the air. The energy was palpable.

Turning to Helga, Louis felt a strange gratitude toward the stranger who'd made the long ride a little less lonely. They shared a quick hug.

"All right, see you later, yeah?" Helga said, clutching her purple bag.

"For sure. I'll text you later and let you know how it goes," Louis replied, giving her a thumbs-up.

With a final wave, they went their separate ways, promising to check in later.

Louis walked through the station, weaving through the crowd and searching for the toilets. He spotted a sign and headed downstairs to the public restrooms, slipping a twenty-pence coin into the barrier slot to enter. Inside, the air smelled of soap, cologne, and the rush of travellers.

He set his bag on the edge of the sink, rummaging through for his essentials—his toothbrush, deodorant, fresh clothes, and hair gel. Quickly brushing his teeth, he studied himself in the mirror, feeling fresher. Grabbing his outfit, he slipped into one of the cramped cubicles. It was a tight squeeze, but he managed, pulling on his black jeans and the jumper his Mum had given him for his eighteenth birthday.

After changing, he returned to the sink to style his hair with gel, smoothing it into place with care. After a final deodorant spray, he looked up at his reflection—ready for the day ahead.

Glancing at his phone, he pulled directions to Escape Hunt in Reading—first stop: a short walk across the road to Victoria train station.

He noticed the change in the atmosphere as soon as he stepped into the underground. People moved cautiously, many wearing masks, others glancing around nervously. Signs plastered the walls, reminders about the virus: **"Remember to Keep Your Distance," "Wear a Mask,"** and **"Practice Good Hygiene."** The scent of hand sanitiser lingered in the air.

Even outside the station, he had noticed the streets felt quieter than he had expected, the bustling crowds smaller. Faces turned down, people giving each other as much space as possible. It starkly contrasted the busy energy of the city he'd seen from the bus. This wasn't the London he had imagined—this was something else.

On the train platform, seats were marked off with black-and-yellow caution tape, and the announcement over the speakers reminded passengers to maintain social distancing. Louis found a seat on the Bakerloo line, a space on either side of him, also taped off.

As the train rumbled along, Louis couldn't shake the feeling of isolation that seemed to hang in the air. Everyone was tucked into their own space, faces hidden behind masks, eyes avoiding each other. A nervous glance was all it took for someone to shrink away. The atmosphere felt tense as if everyone was trying to prevent unseen threats.

It reminded him of a sci-fi movie he'd once watched—one where a virus had taken over the world, and the survivors had to navigate carefully, avoiding the infected. Only this wasn't a movie. This was real.

The train rumbled on, carrying Louis toward Paddington for his connection. He transferred quickly, still feeling a sense of strangeness in the journey.

He climbed the stairs to the upper level at Paddington Station, where his train to Reading was waiting. As he walked through the main concourse, his eyes caught sight of the Paddington Bear gift shop. A wave of nostalgia hit him. His Dad had visited London years ago and brought him a Paddington Bear teddy and a book from this very station. The sight of the same teddy, its blue coat and red hat preserved perfectly in the window stirred a bittersweet mix of emotions—memories of a time when things felt simpler and closer between them. Louis couldn't help but wonder when things had grown so distant between them. He sighed quietly, shaking off the thought. He was here for a reason, and that reason was waiting for him in Reading.

Louis tapped his phone on the barrier and boarded the train. The hum of the tracks soon became the soundtrack to his thoughts.

He found a window seat on the train, slipped in his AirPods, and watched the cityscape blur into the countryside. His excitement grew, and he pulled out his notepad to jot down a few questions for the interview. His handwriting was quick but deliberate, capturing his curiosity and the thrill of the adventure ahead. He glanced out the window between scribbles, a small smile tugging at his lips as the landscape shifted around him.

He checked the time: 10:15 a.m. He thought his Mum should be awake by now. He tapped her name on his phone and, after a couple of rings, heard her voice.

"Hi, Mum! Just wanted to let you know I've arrived safely," he said, picturing her sipping her morning coffee.

"Oh, thank goodness, Louis!" Her voice was filled with a mix of relief and excitement. "I've hardly slept a wink! I know it's silly, but I couldn't stop thinking about you."

Louis chuckled softly. "I met someone on the bus—Helga. We had a good chat, and the ride went faster. Paddington Station… brought back so many memories. I even saw the Paddington Bear shop."

"Oh, Louis, you carried that bear everywhere when you were little," she laughed. "I'm so proud of you, heading off on this adventure."

"I'm on the train now, Mum. I should be in Reading soon. I'm thinking of grabbing breakfast at a café before the escape room," Louis said, watching the landscape turn from city to green fields.

"That sounds like a good plan. And don't forget to call your Gran—she's been asking about you. She'll be relieved to know you're safe."

"I will," he promised, smiling at her concern.

After hanging up, Louis felt a wave of comfort wash over him. He watched the train gliding through the countryside, imagining how far he'd come. The journey, once entirely of uncertainty, was beginning to feel like the start of something new.

The train conductor's voice interrupted his thoughts as they approached Reading. He grabbed his things, his excitement growing.

Once off the train, Louis spotted a nearby café, its aroma inviting him in. He treated himself to a hot chocolate and a croissant, savouring the warmth of the drink and the moment. This pause in an unfamiliar place felt liberating, grounding him before the day's adventure continued.

Remembering Mum's reminder to call Gran, he dialled her number. After a couple of rings, Gran's voice came through, as warm and familiar as ever.

"Hello, my lovely boy!"

"Hi, Gran! Just wanted to let you know I'm safe and in Reading now," he said, sitting in the quiet café, comforted by her voice.

"Oh, I was hoping you'd call! I've been thinking about you all morning. How's it going, love? Are you enjoying yourself?"

"It's… different, Gran," Louis replied, looking around at the signs and empty seats, the weight of the pandemic still evident in the space around him. "There are signs everywhere, so many people wearing masks. Even on the train, half the seats are taped off. I didn't expect it to feel like this."

There was a pause, and then Gran's voice softened with concern. "Yes, it's spreading fast. They've been talking about it nonstop on the news. But you're being careful, aren't you?"

"I am, Gran. Everyone's being cautious. It's like the whole place is on edge," Louis reassured her.

"I do worry," she said, her voice full of care. "But just take things one step at a time".

Louis felt a pang of homesickness but pushed it aside. "I will, Gran. Don't worry," he said, the warmth of her words wrapping around him. "I stopped by Paddington Station earlier. Do you remember that bear Dad got me? They still have the shop there."

"Of course, I remember!" Gran laughed, the fondness in her voice evident. "You carried that bear everywhere until it was falling apart. Are you still carrying him around?"

"Not quite," Louis chuckled. "But I did think of him."

"Good lad," Gran said warmly. "Make sure you have fun today. And call your old Gran occasionally. I love hearing from you."

"I will, Gran. Love you."

"Love you too, dear. Take care of yourself," she said before the line went quiet.

Louis hung up, a small smile on his face. Gran's words lingered with him—comforting, grounding him as he set out toward his next adventure.

The streets of Reading buzzed with life, and Louis moved with purpose, following his phone map towards Escape Hunt, his anticipation building with each step. The building was unassuming, but to Louis, it felt like the gateway to something significant. He stood outside, taking it all in before he stepped inside.

CHAPTER FIVE
UNLOCKING THE FUTURE

Inside, The building was dimly lit, with Doctor Who memorabilia and posters on every wall. Daleks, Cybermen, and various Doctors stared back at him, their presence both daunting and comforting. A young receptionist looked up from her desk and greeted him with a friendly smile.

"Hi there, welcome to Escape Hunt! Are you here for the Doctor Who room?" Louis grinned, pulling out his phone – the invitation email open on the screen.

"I'm here for the interview with Nicholas Briggs." Her eyes lit up.

"Ah, you must be Louis! Mr. Briggs will be thrilled to see you. He's just getting set up in the lounge. Feel free to look around; he'll be out in a few minutes."

Louis nodded his thanks and wandered around, his gaze drifting to a display case holding a replica of the TARDIS key with a plaque that read, "The Key to All of Time and Space." He found himself smiling at the thought: today's experience would be the key to his future.

A few minutes later, he heard footsteps. He turned and saw Nicholas Briggs himself, a man with silvery hair, a warm smile, and an energy that made him seem approachable and wise. Louis had seen him on Doctor Who panels, but he had a casual charm in person.

"Louis! Great to meet you," Briggs said, his voice carrying the rich timbre that had breathed life into the Daleks. He extended a hand, which Louis shook eagerly. "Ready for today?"

"Absolutely," Louis replied, doing his best to sound calm though he was buzzing with excitement. "Thank you so much for the chance."

"Well, it's always a pleasure to meet a new fan and fellow storyteller," Briggs said with a chuckle. "Shall we grab a seat?" They settled into a cosy corner of the lounge, and Louis pulled out his notepad, his fingers already itching to capture every word.

"So, how did you first get involved with Doctor Who?" he began, sticking to his prepared questions to ease into the conversation.

Briggs smiled, leaning back. "Ah, that was ages ago. I've loved the show since I was a kid. I even used to make voice recordings of the monsters! Eventually, I got the opportunity to join as the voice of the Daleks, and, well… once a Dalek, always a Dalek, I suppose."

They talked quickly from there, Briggs sharing behind-the-scenes stories, the art of voicing iconic villains, and the pressure of staying true to the spirit of Doctor Who while bringing fresh life to each character. Louis felt himself relaxing, asking more about Briggs's thoughts on storytelling, fan connections, and how Doctor Who had transformed over the years.

Briggs spoke with genuine passion, his stories vividly bringing the Doctor Who world to life. As they wrapped up, Briggs gestured to a staff member nearby, "How about we capture this memory?"

Louis grinned. "Absolutely!"

The staff member took a photo of Briggs and Louis, smiling side by side, with the TARDIS key display behind them. Louis knew he'd treasure this photo—a symbol of the day his journalistic journey began.

"Now, are you up for the escape room?" Briggs asked, his eyes twinkling.

"Definitely!" Louis replied.

A staff member handed Louis a replica sonic screwdriver, its weight solid and reassuring in his hand. Just as he was about to enter the escape room, he noticed another figure approaching— tall, with glasses, wearing a Doctor Who hoodie, and carrying a camera. Louis blinked in recognition; it was George Sheard, one of his favourite Doctor Who YouTubers, whose reviews and commentary he'd been watching for years.

"George" Louis stammered, wide-eyed. "Wow! I didn't know you'd be here!"

George grinned, just as surprised. "Briggs mentioned another fan was here to interview him. I was hoping we'd meet each other."

Louis felt a thrill of excitement. Here he was, about to do a Doctor Who escape room with his favourite YouTuber. The surreal-ness hit him hard, but George was so friendly and easy-going that the jitters faded quickly. "Let's show this Dalek who's boss!" George said, nodding toward the escape room door. Together, they stepped inside, ready for the challenge.

The room was designed to look like a spaceship control room, with flashing lights, intricate switches, and screens that lit up as soon as the door closed. The countdown clock started ticking, and Nicholas Briggs's deep, Dalek voice suddenly echoed through the room.

"You have twenty minutes to escape or face *extermination!*"

Louis and George shared a look of delight before diving into the puzzles. They tore through clues and deciphered codes, working in sync as they flipped switches, pieced together mysterious symbols, and pulled open hidden compartments. George's enthusiasm and ability made the experience even more fun, and Louis found himself letting loose, enjoying every second.

As the countdown hit two minutes, they solved the final puzzle, triggering the door to unlock with a loud click. They shared a triumphant grin and high-fived, stepping out of the room just as Briggs entered to congratulate them.

"Impressive teamwork!" he said with a grin. "You two could give the Doctor a run for his money."

Louis laughed, still buzzing with adrenaline. "Thanks, Mr. Briggs! And, honestly, this was even better than I imagined."

Briggs chuckled. "Glad to hear it. And call me Nick, would you?" They took one last photo, the three of them—Louis, George, and Briggs—with Louis holding the sonic screwdriver as they all posed in front of the TARDIS key. With promises to stay in touch, they parted ways, and Louis headed back to the train station, his mind a whirlwind of excitement and ideas.

On the train back, Louis texted Helga, eager to share the day's events.

I finished my interview with Nick Briggs—and you won't believe it, but I met George Sheard too! We did the escape room together. I can't wait to tell you all about it!

Her response came quickly:

That's incredible, Louis! I can't wait to hear all about it.

As the train rolled out of Reading, Louis leaned back, content, scribbling his thoughts into his notebook, already crafting the article he'd write.

As Louis stepped into Victoria Station, the lively atmosphere buzzed around him, but his heart raced in anticipation of seeing his newfound friend, Helga, again. Spotting her by the main entrance, leaning casually against a pillar with her bright curls catching the light, a smile spread across her face as soon as she noticed him.

"Hey, Louis!" she called, her voice warm and inviting. "I've been waiting to hear all about your day!"

"Hi, Helga!" Louis responded, his words tumbling out in his eagerness to share. "You won't believe the amazing things that happened!"

They made their way to a cosy pub just a short walk away. The lively atmosphere inside offered a welcoming escape. They found a small table in the corner, where they ordered pink gin and lemonade. The refreshing drinks perfectly matched the evening vibe.

Louis felt that sense of camaraderie blooming between them again, as they clinked their glasses. "Cheers to new adventures!" he said, his heart light with happiness.

"Cheers!" Helga replied, her eyes sparkling with enthusiasm.

Once their drinks were nearly finished, Louis pulled out his phone and let Helga listen to the recording of his interview with Nicholas Briggs. As her eyes widened with fascination, he couldn't help but feel a thrill in sharing this project with her.

"This is incredible, Louis!" she exclaimed after the playback, her excitement contagious. "You did an amazing job!"

They exchanged excited chatter, diving into the interview details and his escape room adventure. Their laughter mingled with the ambient hum of the pub, the evening passing by effortlessly.

Soon, it was time to catch the ten o'clock night bus back to Glasgow. The city lights twinkled around them as they returned to the station, casting a warm glow over the evening.

Boarding the bus, they found their seats and settled in, the gentle hum of the engine lulling them into a comfortable rhythm. The journey passed quickly, filled with laughter and light-hearted banter. Louis shared his favourite Doctor Who episodes and talked about his dreams for the future. But as the hours ticked on, his exhaustion caught up with him, and soon, he found himself drifting off, his head resting against the bus window.

He awoke as the bus pulled into Buchanan Bus Station, the first light of morning shining through the windows.

"Home, sweet home," Helga mumbled softly under her breath as she gathered her things, the words of familiar comfort after their long journey.

CHAPTER SIX
MASKS AND MOMENTS

A few days after returning from London, Louis was sprawled on the couch, absentmindedly scrolling through comments on his article about the escape room adventure and his interview with Nicholas Briggs. Although it had only been published a few hours ago, the positive feedback from readers already filled him with a quiet sense of satisfaction. Mum sat at the other end of the couch, her gaze fixed on the television, where a news report was beginning. Mika lay curled up beside Louis, enjoying the warmth of his lap.

Curious, Louis glanced over to see what had caught his Mum's attention. The news anchor's voice grew sombre, and then Boris Johnson appeared on screen, announcing a public address. Mum nudged him gently. "Lou put that down for a second and watch this."

Louis looked up, sensing the weight in his Mum's tone. Johnson's voice was steady but tense as he delivered the news: "From midnight tonight, we will be entering a national lockdown. This decision has not been made lightly…"

His heart sank as he processed the announcement. The freedom and excitement he had felt just days ago in London now seemed like a distant memory. He exchanged a concerned glance with his Mum, who sighed and shook her head, her expression a mixture of sadness and resolve.

"Looks like we'll be staying put for a while, love," she murmured, her voice gentle but carrying the weight of uncertainty. Louis nodded, feeling a strange mix of fear and frustration settle in.

Mika let out a soft whine, sensing the change in the room's mood. Louis absentmindedly scratched behind her ears, grounding himself in the familiar comfort of his loyal companion.

Mum turned to him, her eyes filled with the warmth and steadiness he'd always relied on. "Whatever happens, Louis, we'll get through this together. Let's try to make the best of it, all right?"

He offered her a small smile, trying to mirror her strength. "Yeah, Mum. We'll be okay."

The Prime Minister continued to speak about school closures and the halting of non-essential services, and Louis's stomach dropped when he heard that colleges would be closing as well. College had been his escape, his sanctuary, where he could build his future.

"No college, either," Louis muttered, half to himself. The thought of being cut off from his classmates and radio projects left him feeling suddenly adrift. The college had been more than just a place to learn—it was where he was testing his skills, seeing where his dreams might take him. And now, it all felt like it was on hold.

His phone buzzed, and a flurry of notifications lit up his screen. Messages from his friends flooded in, all echoing the same theme:

Did you see the news, Louis?

This is wild, mate. Everything's shutting down.

No college! What are we supposed to do now?

He sighed, quickly typing out replies, nodding as he read their messages. Everyone felt the same—a mixture of disbelief, worry, and confusion. He paused before sending a message to the group chat, fingers hovering over the screen. What could he say? His mind drifted to all the memories of college—the late nights spent editing, the endless conversations with Megan about their favourite radio personalities, and the excitement of seeing his work come to life.

Just days ago, he had felt on the brink of something big. Now, everything felt like it was slipping away. No late-night edits, no more half-joking, half-serious conversations with Megan, no assignments to dive into. The momentum he'd been building felt like it had vanished, leaving him stuck in limbo.

Mum's hand on his arm brought him back to reality. "I know it feels like the world's upside down, but you'll get back to it eventually," she said softly, her eyes filled with understanding.

"Yeah, I just… it feels like everything's on hold, you know?" Louis murmured, stroking Mika's fur for comfort. "Everything I was building just doesn't matter now."

"Maybe not in the way you're used to, but it still matters, Lou," she said gently, squeezing his shoulder. "You're still that creative, driven person—even if things have to slow down for a while." She paused, her voice softening. "And you've got friends, family. This is just a different chapter."

Louis nodded, feeling some of the tension start to ease. His phone buzzed again, and he glanced down at a message from Megan:

We will get through this together. We're still a team, even if it's on pause.

Seeing her message helped. Louis smiled, sending a quick reply before slipping his phone into his pocket. Maybe he couldn't control how long things would be on pause, but he still had the people around him—and the hope that one day, he'd pick things back up right where he left off.

A little while later, Mum's phone rang, the familiar chime filling the room. She picked it up, and her expression softened when she saw who it was.

"It's Gran," she murmured, answering and pressing the speaker button so Louis could hear too. "Hi, Mum. Louis is here as well—you're on speaker."

"Oh, thank you, love," Gran's voice crackled through, filled with that familiar warmth, but there was a slight tremor beneath it. "I saw the news, and I had to call. I know it will be a while before I can see you both again, and that... that will be hard."

Louis's heart clenched. He'd just been at Gran's house, working in her garden, sharing tea and laughter. The thought that their visits might be put on hold for who knew how long weighed heavily on him.

"We'll be okay, Mum," Mum replied, her tone steady but gentle. "And we'll make sure you are, too. We can call, maybe even video call—it's just for now."

Gran let out a shaky laugh, trying to keep her spirits up. "Yes, I know, dear. But I was looking forward to you both coming by for tea again. It's not the same without you here, rattling about the house alone."

Louis swallowed hard, the sadness in her voice settling deep in his chest. "Gran," he spoke up, trying to make her feel his love. As soon as this is over, we'll be right back there with you—Mika, too. You won't even be able to get us to leave."

"Oh, my dear," Gran replied, her voice softening. "That's all I needed to hear. I'll keep everything ready for when that day comes."

They sat in a brief silence, the weight of the situation pressing down on them. Mum finally broke the quiet. "We love you, Mum. And we'll get through this together, all of us. Don't hesitate to call anytime, all right?"

"I will, I will," Gran said, her tone brightening. "Take care, you two. I'm so lucky to have you. I'll keep the kettle warm."

The call ended, leaving the room quieter and a little heavier. His Mum sighed, rubbing her temples. "It's hard on her, you know, being alone."

Louis nodded, trying to ignore the ache in his chest. "Yeah. She was always there for us… and now, when she needs us most…"

"She's strong, Lou," Mum reassured him, offering a small smile. "And just like she said, we'll be there as soon as this ends."

Louis returned her smile, trying to believe in it fully. For now, it would have to be enough.

As the call lingered in Louis's mind, his Mum glanced at him, her eyes warm. "She's so proud of you, you know," she said softly, breaking the silence. "She mentioned your article to me just yesterday. She told everyone that she'd been bragging about her grandson, the writer."

Louis smiled, a mixture of pride and bashfulness sweeping over him. "Did she?"

"Oh, she did," Mum laughed, her face lighting up. "She's shown it to half her friends—and she asked me to print out a few more copies for her to keep around the house. I think the neighbours know every word of that article by now."

Louis chuckled, the thought of Gran sharing his work filling him with warmth. "I didn't think it would mean that much to her."

Mum's gaze softened, her voice gentle. "She's always seen the best in you, Lou. She knows you're working hard and following your dreams, which means everything to her and me."

"Thanks, Mum." Louis looked down, grateful and emotional. "I guess I never thought it'd reach people like that, especially her friends."

"Well, it has," she replied, reassuringly touching his shoulder. "So don't stop. Keep going, keep writing, keep finding things you love and sharing them with the world. We're all rooting for you."

Louis nodded, a swell of determination rising within him. Despite everything shutting down, he still had this—his family's pride, Gran's unwavering support, and the reminder that his work could touch others in ways he hadn't imagined.

In the first few weeks of lockdown, Louis poured his heart into his blog. Writing had always been his outlet, but now it felt like an anchor, keeping him steady amid the chaos of a world turned upside down. Each post allowed him to capture moments of resilience and connection, preserving them as a reminder of what truly mattered.

Each Thursday, he and his Mum would stand at the backdoor, clapping and cheering for the NHS alongside their neighbours. As he looked around, hearing applause fill the street, he felt a rare sense of unity and hope—small moments that helped him believe life would return to normal. Inspired, he poured these thoughts into his blog. His friends, Karen, Sarah, Lauren, and Carly, had been constant sources of strength and laughter. They had been each other's lifelines, so he dedicated a post to the importance of friendship during lockdown. His article resonated with readers, as did another he wrote on mental health, which brought him a wave of new followers and support. But, as he encouraged others to seek hope, Louis felt a quiet ache inside— one he tried to ignore, pushing it to the background as he focused on helping others.

Despite the occasional high of writing and its satisfaction, a creeping sense of loneliness grew. Louis couldn't help but notice how many people around him were riding out the pandemic with partners. He would see Instagram posts of couples binge-watching shows together, cooking meals side by side, or simply holding each other in a painfully intimate way. The physical and emotional void was hard to ignore.

The days blurred together in a new routine. His nights were spent on FaceTime marathons with Sarah and Karen, their laughter and shared memories stretching into the early hours, offering relief. But at times, he found it hard to shake the nagging emptiness he felt after the calls ended. It was a loneliness that seemed to sit deeper, lingering just under the surface.

He revisited his favourite Doctor Who episodes and posted reviews on his blog. The familiar worlds of time travel and heroism provided an escape, a sense of adventure that he craved. He swore he wouldn't let the dark times drain his creativity, but a creeping sense of fatigue followed him, and he often had to force himself to focus. The emptiness in his heart seemed to grow each day, though he struggled to pinpoint why.

One evening, while taking a writing break, Louis scrolled through Instagram. A Story from Sarah appeared at the top of his feed, and he tapped on it out of habit. His heart clenched when he saw her sitting on a plush sofa, a bowl of popcorn in her lap, smiling at the camera. The caption read: '**Movie night with Paul!**' The following clip showed Paul leaning into the frame, making a silly face that made Sarah laugh.

Louis's chest tightened, a complicated mix of emotions swirling inside him. He felt an itch of jealousy, not just for Sarah being with Paul but also for the intimacy she was experiencing—something he craved so desperately. He wondered, briefly, if things had been different, if Paul had just been honest about who he was, whether that could have been him and Paul together, sharing a movie night, leaning into each other's warmth. But then, just as quickly, he felt a wave of guilt. He was worried about Sarah, afraid that she might end up hurt by Paul, as he knew she would if the truth ever came out. The thought of her heartbreak weighed heavily on him.

He set his phone down, trying to shake off the jealousy and frustration. He had his Mum and was grateful for their bond, but it wasn't the same. It was intimacy he craved—the feeling of being held, kissed, and seen in a way only a partner could. He missed the thrill of connection, the small nights of closeness that had once seemed so easy to find on a night out.

Cooking with Mum became a highlight of his lockdown routine. Every evening, they would gather in the kitchen, armed with new recipes they'd found online or remembered from Gran's dinners. They took turns chopping vegetables, stirring sauces, and experimenting with spices. One night, they made Cajun pasta with a creamy sauce and just the right kick of spice. Next, they attempted homemade Chinese dishes, filling the kitchen with the comforting scent of garlic and soy. Each meal was an adventure, with laughter over failed attempts and high-fives when they nailed a dish.

These nights spent with his Mum felt like a blessing, a chance to strengthen their bond through shared effort and love. Yet, late at night, when the house was quiet, Louis sometimes felt a gnawing sense of sadness, a reminder of his missing connection.

On top of their nightly cooking, they kept their spirits up with regular FaceTime calls to Gran. Though Gran wasn't always a fan of new technology, she adapted quickly, her face lighting up on the screen as they caught up. Louis enjoyed showing her their culinary experiments, even if she laughed at some of their less successful dishes. She'd share her recipes, offering tips from years of experience, with gentle reminders to "add a bit more salt" or "never overcook the pasta." These calls became a cherished routine, bridging the physical distance between them. Even though they couldn't be together, seeing Gran's smile helped Louis feel hopeful.

But Louis couldn't help feeling guilt when he thought about his Dad's side of the family. His Dad's Mum—Louis's other Gran—was in a care home. He still hadn't heard from his Dad in a long while and knew little about how she was holding up during the pandemic. The idea of her isolation, away from family, weighed on him. He wanted to reach out to his Dad to check in on her, but their relationship had grown so distant, and he worried it might only add to the confusion and pain he was already feeling. The silence between them felt heavier than ever, a reminder of how much had been left unsaid.

Weeks turned to months, and the news only grew darker. Each new headline about rising cases cast a shadow, and Louis found it more challenging to hold onto hope. Then, one morning, he received an email from his college: classes would continue online. The change was bittersweet. He missed the energy of being on campus, the chance to bounce ideas off classmates and engage in discussions that sparked his creativity. At least, he thought, he could reconnect with his classmates and keep pursuing his goals—though part of him couldn't shake the thought that it would all feel hollow without being there in person.

The college soon adapted to online learning, and logging into his classes each day quickly became part of Louis's new routine. Though online learning felt much more complicated than being in the actual classroom, it offered a touch of familiarity in an otherwise uncertain time. Seeing his lecturers, classmates, and especially Megan, even if only through a video call, was a comfort. Their faces, appearing in little squares on his screen, reminded him of the usual rhythms of his life before lockdown. Yet each call felt slightly off as if he saw them from a distance beyond just a computer screen. He struggled to focus, often feeling himself drift into thoughts of simpler days when college had felt like a second home.

The online sessions presented new challenges—technical issues, distractions at home, and the absence of the hands-on, collaborative energy they once shared in person. Louis appreciated any connection he could find, but some days felt like he was merely going through the motions. He missed the buzz of the campus studio, the energy that once filled him with excitement and a sense of purpose. Now, a quiet emptiness shadowed even his best efforts.

Louis continued tackling the challenges of online learning. It wasn't easy—he missed the camaraderie, structure, and sense of accomplishment that came from tackling projects side by side with his classmates. But with each assignment and Zoom session, he found a way to keep going, clinging to the reminder of his goals and the passion that had driven him to start the course.

On the most challenging days, when motivation wavered, he leaned on his friends and family. Sarah and Karen, his FaceTime regulars, became his study buddies from afar, offering encouragement and sharing study tips over calls. Megan would shoot him quick messages, checking in and reminding him he wasn't alone in feeling the weight.

His Mum continued to be a source of strength, often bringing him a cup of tea during his study sessions, her presence a quiet encouragement. Gran would call him before deadlines, cheering him on with stories of her persistence and pushing through tough times. These moments were a balm to Louis's heart, though he knew he was only managing to keep himself from feeling overwhelmed.

As summer approached, Louis could feel the weight of his efforts beginning to pay off. Bit by bit, he chipped away at his coursework, finishing each assignment, one Zoom session at a time. He'd seen more of his classmates' bedrooms than he ever thought he would, and while it was not the college experience he had envisioned, it was something—a shared effort to make the best of things.

Finally, as June arrived, Louis received the email he had been waiting for: he had passed his course. Relief washed over him as he read the words, and for the first time in what felt like forever, he let himself exhale, a wide grin spreading across his face.

He raced downstairs, practically bursting into the kitchen where Mum was preparing lunch. "I did it, Mum!" he said, unable to hold back his excitement.

Her face lit up, and she wrapped him in a tight hug. "Oh, Lou! I knew you would! You worked so hard—you deserve this."

As they celebrated together, Louis felt a swell of pride and gratitude. Despite everything that had happened, he'd made it through, supported by the people who believed in him every step of the way. That summer was finally here, and although he didn't know what lay ahead, he knew he'd faced one of the toughest challenges of his life—and come out stronger on the other side.

As Louis and his Mum celebrated his passing, the excitement was already sparking ideas for what they could do now that lockdown restrictions had started to ease, even if only slightly. Beaming with pride, Mum couldn't hold back a little extra bit of news.

"Oh, and Louis," she said excitedly, "there's something else. They just announced we're allowed one visitor from another household as long as it's outside and we stay distanced."

Louis's face lit up immediately. "Wait—does that mean Gran can come to visit?"

She nodded, grinning. "Yes! We could set up a little spot in the garden, make it nice and cosy. I've already told her, and she can't wait to see you."

The thought of seeing Gran in person made his heart soar. After months of FaceTime calls and phone conversations, the chance to sit with her, even just for an hour or two, felt like a gift. The familiar ache of missing her was suddenly replaced with anticipation as he thought about all the stories she'd have to share and the chance to hear them face to face.

"She's over the moon about it," his Mum added with a laugh. "I think she's already planning the snacks she'll bring over, even if we're just sitting at opposite ends of the garden."

Louis smiled, the vision of Gran sitting with them, laughing in the summer sun, filling him with hope. It wasn't exactly back to normal, but it was something. And for now, that was more than enough.

The day Gran arrived was bright and clear, a hopeful summer morning. Louis was up early, helping Mum set up chairs and fluff cushions in the back garden. They'd created a cosy spot near the lilac bushes where the dogs could roam freely, and Louis set out a small table with tea and biscuits. His Mum's Garden, in full bloom, was a riot of colour— a stark contrast to the months they'd spent inside.

When Gran's car pulled up outside, Louis felt excited. He hadn't realized how much he missed her until now. As she stepped out, adjusting her mask and straightening her cardigan, her eyes crinkled with happiness.

Gran quickened her steps toward the garden, and when she saw him, her eyes welled up with tears. She pulled off her gloves and dabbed at her cheeks. "Oh, Louis... my boy..." she said, voice thick with emotion. "It's been so long."

Louis felt his throat tighten. "We missed you so much, Gran," he whispered. "Feels like forever."

Gran nodded; eyes soft. "It's like seeing you for the first time again." She smiled beneath her mask. "You've gotten taller, I swear."

He laughed. "Maybe an inch."

Mum urged them to sit. "Come on, let's sit before we all start blubbering," she teased, though her eyes were bright. Mika and Gran's dogs began running circles around each other, tails wagging excitedly.

As they settled, Gran gave Louis a scrutinizing look. "Louis, dear, you're starting to look like one of those Beatles. That mop of hair... John Lennon, is it?" She raised an eyebrow.

Louis rolled his eyes, grinning. "Yeah, it's getting wild. But with hairdressers still closed, it's like the world's paused anything non-essential."

Mum laughed. "If this goes on much longer, I'll have to take matters into my own hands. I could give you a quick trim myself."

Louis raised his eyebrows in mock horror. "Right, Mum. You'll grab the dog clippers and give me a full buzz cut."

Gran laughed, patting his hand. "Well, at least it would be low maintenance. And it'll grow back. Maybe you're meant to be the next Beatle."

They all laughed as they settled into their chairs, sipping tea while the dogs ran around. Gran's eyes roamed the garden, taking in the blooming flowers. "This is lovely," she said, her gaze soft. "Your Mum's Garden feels like a little slice of heaven."

Louis's mother smiled. "It's my therapy," she admitted. It helps me get through the weeks."

After a while, Gran leaned forward, her voice quieter. "I hear they're talking about a vaccine soon," she said. "Could be a way out of all this."

Louis nodded. "Yeah, the government says it'll take time to get to everyone, but it's something to hold on to."

Gran's eyes brightened. "I'll take any scrap of hope they're handing out if it means things can go back to normal" she replied.

His Mum leaned forward, serious. "Maybe even better than normal. This has taught us what's truly important—family, friends, being present…"

Gran nodded, her gaze shifting to the dogs as they wrestled in the grass. "And I'll never take any of this for granted again. Just sitting here with you both…" She paused, dabbing at her eyes. "It's a gift."

Louis felt a tightness in his chest. His mind wandered to his other Gran, isolated in her care home. He imagined her, sitting alone, cut off from everyone.

"Mum," he said quietly, glancing at her. "I can't help thinking about my Dad's Mum. In that care home with no family, no friends… I can't imagine what that's like."

Mum's face softened, and she touched his arm. "It's tough, Lou. No one should have to go through that kind of loneliness."

Gran nodded in understanding. "Your Gran is strong. I know it must be hard on her, but she will know you're thinking of her. When it's safe, you'll see her again one day."

Louis smiled weakly, his heart aching. The months of isolation had taken a toll, and though he'd tried to stay positive, some days felt harder than others. Today, seeing his Gran in person, he felt the weight of those worries.

Gran must have sensed it. She reached out, her hand close to his. "Lou, it's okay to feel sad. We've all been through so much. It's normal to miss people, to wonder when things will feel right again."

Louis took a deep breath. "Yeah, I've tried to keep it together, but sometimes I miss everything. All the things we took for granted."

"We're all carrying something heavy, Louis. It's okay to feel lost or sad—what matters is we're here for each other." Mum responded.

A few minutes passed as they sat together, the weight of everything they'd been through feeling lighter in shared silence. They laughed about the little things they missed—impromptu coffee dates, movie nights, the simple freedom of going out without fear. Gran shared stories of weekends at the seaside and walks under the stars.

The dogs finally tired out as the afternoon stretched on, lying in the shade. Gran leaned back, a contented look on her face as she gazed at the sky.

"It'll get better," she said softly.

"The world's still a beautiful place. We just need a little more patience."

CHAPTER SEVEN
THE PRICE OF CONNECTION

Halfway through summer- news that would give Louis a bit of normality back broke - pubs across the UK could reopen, but only under strict rules: table service, social distancing, a 10 PM curfew, and no nightclubs. Louis felt a strange mix of excitement and dread at the announcement. It was a taste of normalcy, warped by the new reality. The idea of seeing his friends in a familiar setting was too tempting to resist, so they quickly made plans. Carly, Karen, and Lauren would meet him at First Ed. Sarah declined, saying she was going on a date with Paul, whom she'd been seeing more of during lockdown. Initially, Louis was surprised but brushed it off, focusing on the night ahead.

By five, he was at First Ed, surrounded by a buzz of eager patrons reclaiming a slice of their former lives. The pub was full, but the energy felt different. Servers flitted between tables, patrons sat spaced apart, and the usual hum of chatter was quieter than ever.

Despite the 10 PM curfew and table service rules, Louis, Carly, Karen, and Lauren soaked in the atmosphere, clinking glasses, laughing, and reminiscing about nights that once felt so ordinary. "Feels surreal, doesn't it?" Carly said, swirling her drink. "Like we're in some parallel universe where nights out are... sanitized."

"Honestly, we're practically in a sci-fi movie," Karen quipped, raising her glass in a mock toast. They all laughed, clinking glasses together.

Louis grinned, leaning back in his chair. "I've missed this. Missed us."

For a while, the curfew and masks faded into the background. They talked about everything—memories from pre-COVID nights out to the strange ambitions they'd developed during lockdown. The connection they shared felt like a reminder of everything they had lost and everything they were starting to reclaim.

When the last orders were called, the group lingered, reluctant to leave. The thought of heading back to empty rooms felt unbearable. Karen, sensing the restless energy, leaned in with a mischievous glint in her eye. "All right, so... I know a guy throwing an afters who might have some party favours if we want to keep this going."

Louis felt a rush of excitement. It had been long since they'd let loose and felt genuinely free. They all agreed eagerly, piling into a cab. The buzz of alcohol mixed with anticipation, and the night ahead felt like a long-awaited release.

At the flat, Karen made her way over to a guy leaning against the wall. After a quick exchange, she returned with a handful of small, pink pills, passing them around.

Carly held hers up thoughtfully. "Here's to being alive," she said, grinning as she swallowed it.

"To freedom," Louis echoed, swallowing his pill. A shiver ran through him as it dissolved, and within moments, the room softened. A warmth spread through his chest, the music pulsing in time with his heartbeat, louder and more vibrant than he'd heard in months.

He looked around, seeing his friends anew. Lauren was giggling at something Carly had whispered while Karen swayed to the music, a serene smile on her face.

"Oh my god," Louis murmured to Karen, his smile wide. "I forgot how incredible this feels."

"I know, right?" Karen grinned, eyes sparkling. "Nights like these... they're what keep us going."

They moved to the makeshift dance floor, laughing, twirling in time with the beat. The music lifted them, binding them together in pure joy. Every beat was a reminder of what they'd lost and reclaimed, a shared celebration of resilience.

Louis felt alive, his senses heightened, every touch electric. He looked around at Carly, Karen, and Lauren, feeling a deep connection with them, a bond that went beyond words.

As they danced, Louis caught sight of Paul arriving with some mates. A mix of surprise, curiosity, and a hint of jealousy stirred in him. He overheard Paul's friends asking about his date with Sarah, but Louis tried to ignore it, pushing through the moment with forced casualness.

Later, while catching his breath in the corner of the flat, Louis saw Paul moving through the crowd. Their eyes met, and Paul made his way over with a slow smile, exuding confidence.

Louis tried to ignore the flutter of nerves in his stomach. "Didn't expect to see you here," Paul said, his voice smooth as he scanned Louis's face.

"Yeah?" Louis managed; his voice unsteady. They chuckled, the tension between them growing thicker with each word.

Paul glanced around. "Look, I've got a room free if you want to... talk somewhere quieter. No one would have to know. Sarah won't find out."

Louis's heart raced. He thought of Sarah, but in the haze of alcohol and pills, his resolve faltered. "I shouldn't. Sarah's my friend," he murmured, his voice lacking conviction.

"Come on," Paul whispered, close enough that Louis could feel his breath. "It's just one night. No one needs to know."

Louis hesitated, torn between loyalty and the promise of excitement. In the blur of the night, his need for connection overpowered his guilt. He nodded, and they moved to a spare room at the back of the flat, closing the door softly behind them.

In the dim room, the music faded into the background as they collided, laughing softly, pulled together by a whirlwind of desire. Louis's pulse quickened as Paul's lips met his—slow, then urgent. Every touch and kiss sparked an intense rush, drowning out everything else.

Clothes came off in a blur, and Louis found himself breathless as he traced the lines of Paul's toned body. The attraction was undeniable, and he couldn't help but feel drawn to every inch of Paul's physique.

Paul noticed the way Louis's gaze lingered, a grin tugging at his lips. "Like the view?" he murmured, pulling Louis closer. He leaned in, pressing a trail of heated kisses along Louis's neck, moving slowly, savouring the moment.

In a tangle of limbs, they fell onto the bed, their bodies intertwining as they gave in to the heat between them. Louis felt utterly consumed by the closeness, the warmth of Paul's skin against his, the intoxicating scent of him filling his senses. They moved in sync, a rhythm dictated by need and desire, their breaths heavy, mingling in the close space. Every touch, every kiss felt like a release of the loneliness and isolation they had both carried in silence.

As they lay there afterwards, their bodies entangled, breaths slowly evening out, Louis felt a strange mix of contentment and regret settling in. He turned to look at Paul, hoping for reassurance, something to make sense of what had just happened, but Paul's face was unreadable, his gaze fixed on a distant point in the room. The closeness that had been there just minutes ago seemed to slip away, leaving a hollow quiet in its place.

After a long silence, Paul sat up, breaking their gaze. "Guess I should get back out there," he said, his tone casual, as if the intensity they'd shared had already faded.

But Louis couldn't shake the nagging thoughts clouding his mind. As Paul moved to pull him closer for a final kiss, Louis found himself searching for something more than the thrill—a hint that maybe, just maybe, Paul felt the same connection he did.

Breathlessly, Louis pulled back, studying Paul's face. "Paul... this thing with Sarah... what are you doing with her?"

Paul shrugged, a smirk tugging at the corner of his mouth. "It's just a bit of fun," he murmured, brushing a strand of Louis's hair back. "It's not serious. She doesn't need to know about this."

Louis's stomach tightened, a flicker of disappointment gnawing at him. "But she thinks it is. You're practically dating her."

Paul's smirk faded, replaced by a guarded expression. "She's my mate, yeah. But... this with you... it's different." He looked away, the confident mask slipping briefly. "It's easier this way."

Louis's frustration surged, his heart pounding with longing and exasperation. "Why can't you just be honest?" His voice was barely a whisper. "About who you are."

Paul's jaw tightened. "It's complicated, all right?" he muttered, his tone low. "People don't get it. It's not as simple as you think, Louis."

Louis's head shook, a sense of hurt building in his chest. "It doesn't have to be so complicated. I wish... I wish you'd let yourself be real with me. Just for once."

Paul's eyes softened, and Louis thought he saw a flicker of vulnerability—the person he so severely wanted Paul to be. But it vanished just as quickly, replaced by the familiar guarded look. "Look, I like you, all right?" Paul murmured, brushing his fingers across Louis's cheek. "But what we have... it's different. It's something I don't want to ruin by overthinking it."

Louis swallowed; his heart heavy with words he couldn't say. "I just don't want to keep hiding," he admitted. "Every time we're together, it feels amazing, but then I'm left feeling... I don't know... disposable."

Paul's fingers tightened gently on his shoulder, his gaze steady. "You're not disposable," he whispered. "But this is how it has to be. I can't give you anything else, Louis. Not now."

Louis's chest tightened as he accepted the truth: despite everything they'd shared, Paul would keep him at arm's length, still hiding behind his fears. The connection Louis craved—open, honest, and vulnerable—was something Paul wasn't ready to give.

"So... what now?" Louis asked, his voice barely audible.

Paul took a long breath, running a hand through his hair. "We go back out there, laugh, keep it casual. Like it's always been." He paused, meeting Louis's gaze with an intensity that almost made Louis believe things could be different. "No need to complicate it, yeah?"

Louis managed a weak nod, his heart sinking. "Yeah... I get it."

Paul leaned in, pressing one last kiss to his forehead before pulling away, his hand slipping from Louis's as he rose to get dressed.

Louis watched him dress quickly, an indifferent smile on Paul's face as he fastened his belt and slipped out the door, leaving him alone in the dim room. A strange emptiness settled over him as Paul's voice echoed faintly from the hallway. "I'll see you out there," he called, the casual tone slipping back into his voice. The door clicked shut, and Louis was left in the silence, the weight of what had happened pressing down on him.

As he lay back, he stared up at the ceiling, his pulse finally slowing as the thrill of the night faded, giving way to a weight he hadn't expected. The haze of euphoria dissolved, replaced by a gnawing guilt that clawed at him. He'd wanted this moment with Paul for so long—a glimpse of something real between them— but now, all he felt was regret.

He thought of Sarah, her easy smile, their trust, and a sick feeling twisted in his gut. Sarah had been kind to him, standing by his side through every awkward phase and challenging day. And he'd just crossed a line he knew she would never forgive if she found out.

A wave of shame washed over him; sharper than any thrill he'd felt moments before. He pictured Sarah's face if she ever knew the truth, the hurt and betrayal that would flicker across her features. She'd trusted him—and he'd let his feelings and confusion drive him to betray that trust.

As he lay there in the quiet, he realised he had not just lost a piece of himself tonight; he'd risked losing one of the few people who truly knew him. The hollow ache in his chest settled deeper, and he turned onto his side, unable to shake the feeling that whatever had happened in that room, whatever he felt for Paul, the price was far too high.

The silence pressed down on him, unforgiving, and he couldn't escape the sinking truth: he had traded something real, something honest with Sarah, for a fleeting hook-up with someone who couldn't even be honest with him. As he closed his eyes, all he could see was her face—innocent, trusting, and utterly unaware of the choice he'd made.

When morning came, Karen and Carly found him still in the spare room, curled up in bed. They didn't ask questions; they just gave him a knowing look and helped him gather his things.

"You, okay?" Carly asked gently as they stepped outside into the soft morning light.

"Yeah," he mumbled, though his stomach churned, and he could feel the weight of his choices pressing down on him.

As they walked in silence, the morning felt calm and surreal, a strange contrast to the hazy chaos of the night before. Louis's mind replayed every moment with Paul—every heated glance, every laugh they shared, and every kiss that had felt electric at the time. But now, in the cold light of day, all he felt was a growing ache of regret and the bitter edge of guilt twisting inside him.

Carly broke the silence with a sigh, nudging him playfully. "Last night was... something else, huh?"

Louis managed a weak smile. "Yeah. Something else."

Karen laughed, though her voice had a slight slur from the remnants of their night. "We needed that. After all these months of lockdown, we were caged animals or something. Last night... it was like we were alive again, right?"

Louis nodded absently, though he felt anything but alive now. In the light of day, the night's euphoria seemed dulled, overshadowed by the reality of what he'd done and the betrayal that came with it.

They reached a crossroads where their paths would diverge. Carly gave him a quick hug. "Get some rest, all right?"

Louis smiled and waved as they left, but the weight in his chest grew heavier as he turned toward home. He knew he had to confront his feelings—and his mind kept returning to Sarah. How could he look her in the eye now? What would she say if she knew?

That night, he sat cross-legged on his bed, listening to Taylor Swift's folklore. Illicit Affairs played softly, each lyric tightening the ache he'd been carrying for days. The song cut painfully close, echoing everything he felt about Paul—moments stolen in secret, the longing, and the guilt of knowing it couldn't last.

He tugged at the frayed edge of his duvet, trying to blink away tears as memories rushed in: Paul's touch, the way everything else faded when they were close. But it was complicated—Paul was with Sarah, one of his best friends, and the weight felt unbearable. Louis understood why Paul was scared to come out, yet it didn't dull the hurt.

A gentle knock at the door snapped him out of his thoughts. He pulled out an Air Pod and wiped his face. "Come in."

Mum stepped in, holding a plate of macaroni mince—her go-to comfort dish. She offered him a warm, knowing smile. "Dinner's ready," she said, her voice soft. "Thought you might want to eat in here tonight."

117

Louis forced a small smile as he took the plate. "Thanks, Mum."

She sat down beside him, her gaze flickering over his face. "You've been quiet. Everything all right?"

He hesitated, then shrugged. "Yeah, just... thinking."

She nodded, then sighed. "Looks like another lockdown might be coming. Cases are going up again."

Louis's stomach twisted. The thought of more isolation, more days blurring together, felt unbearable. "Great," he muttered, poking at his food. "Just what we needed."

She squeezed his shoulder. "I know. But we got through it before. We'll get through it again."

They sat together momentarily, letting the silence settle before she gently changed the subject. "Have you thought any more about applying for your next course, the journalism one?"

He sighed, pushing his fork around his plate. "I don't know. Online learning has been rough. I might wait until things are back on campus."

She gave him an understanding smile. "Just promise me you won't give up on your dreams."

"Yeah, I'll think about it," he mumbled.

She gave him a reassuring nod. "Come down when you're ready. I was thinking Star Wars tonight.

Later, Louis joined her and Mika on the couch. 'Star Wars: The Phantom Menace' was already cued up, and Mika wagged her tail as he sat beside her. She let out a slight cough, and Louis frowned.

"She's been doing that a lot lately," he said, glancing at his Mum.

She nodded, concern crossing her face. "If it gets worse, I'll call the vet."

Louis scratched Mika behind the ears, feeling a pang of worry. She'd always been a comfort, especially during times like these. As the movie began, he tried to focus, but his thoughts drifted back to Paul and everything he'd been bottling up.

Finally, he paused the movie and turned to look at Mum, his voice hesitant. "Mum... can I talk to you about something?"

Her expression softened. "Of course, Lou. What's on your mind?"

He took a deep breath and explained. He told her about his history with Paul, their connection before Paul and Sarah were together, and the night things had gone too far. The guilt weighed heavily on him, knowing he'd hurt both Sarah - and himself.

Mum listened without interrupting; her face full of understanding. When he finished, she took his hand. "Oh, Lou. I'm so sorry you're going through this. It sounds painful."

Louis blinked back tears. "I feel so guilty, Mum. Sarah's one of my best friends, and Paul... he's too scared to come out. But I still have feelings for him, and it just hurts."

She pulled him into a hug. "It's okay to feel hurt and confused. Your feelings are real. But you're right—you must be

119

honest with yourself and Sarah. Holding all this in isn't fair to anyone."

Louis let the tears fall, the weight of everything pressing down on him. "I just wish things could return to normal," he whispered.

"I know," she said softly. "But whatever happens, I'm here. We'll get through this together."

Louis managed a small, broken laugh through his tears. "Thanks, Mum."

She smiled, brushing his hair back. "Always. Now, shall we get back to the pod racing?"

Louis smiled back and let the movie continue. He let himself get lost in it for a while, feeling more grounded. Life was still messy, but he had Mum, Mika, his Gran, and a sense of hope that maybe things would be okay.

Mika let out another slight cough, and Mum looked down at her, frowning slightly. "If this keeps up, we'll get her checked out," she said gently.

CHAPTER EIGHT
HEART MURMURS

The following day, Louis sat on a stool in the bathroom, a towel draped over his shoulders as Mum flicked on the clippers. She gave him a playful grin. "Ready for your professional cut, Mr. Lennon?"

He chuckled. "Just don't shave off an eyebrow, all right?"

She rolled her eyes. "I could be quite the stylist if I wanted to," she teased. "Now sit still."

The buzzing filled the room, and Louis watched his hair fall in clumps onto the towel. His Mum tilted his head this way and that, taking her work seriously but with an amused smile. They laughed whenever the clippers snagged on a stubborn bit, sharing glances in the mirror.

"Who needs a salon?" she said, winking. "I'm practically a pro."

"Totally," Louis replied with a smirk. "You could add 'amateur barber' to your CV."

"Careful," she joked. "Or I'll leave you with a bald patch."

When she finished, Louis looked at himself in the mirror, surprised. The buzz cut wasn't half bad, and he felt lighter—almost free.

"Well?" she asked, grinning.

He nodded approvingly. "Not bad at all. Guess I'll book you in every few weeks."

They cleaned up, chatting and joking about her new barber skills. It felt like a simple, comforting moment—something he hadn't realised he needed.

But then Mika, resting nearby, let out a harsher cough and wobbled unsteadily. Louis's Mum immediately knelt beside her, worry creasing her face. "Poor thing," she murmured, steadying Mika. "I'll call the vet today."

Louis's stomach twisted as he scratched Mika's ears, the lightness of the moment replaced with concern. But as he looked at his Mum, he felt a flicker of gratitude for these small comforts—a reminder that, despite everything, he wasn't alone.

Later that day, Louis's friends planned another night out, but his heart wasn't in it. The invitation went out to Sarah too, but she replied that she'd be staying at Paul's flat, a message that hit Louis like a punch to the gut. The guilt he'd tried to push down now churned with jealousy and frustration. He thought of all the times he and Sarah had confided in each other, their years of friendship, and a heavy shame settled in his chest. He couldn't pretend things were every day—not if he ever wanted to look Sarah in the eye again.

Pacing his bedroom, he wrestled with the truth he'd been holding back. It wasn't just about last week at the afters; it was about everything between him and Paul, dating back to that night before COVID. Heart pounding, he texted Sarah, asking her to meet him at the park – before setting off to meet her.

When Sarah arrived, she looked worried, her brow knit as she sat on the bench. "Louis, what's going on? You look terrible."

Louis sat beside her, head lowered, searching for the right words. He'd replayed this conversation a hundred times, but now that she was in front of him, it felt impossible. "Sarah, I... I need to tell you something about Paul."

She frowned, leaning in. "What are you talking about?"

Taking a shaky breath, Louis forced himself to meet her gaze. "There's more going on with Paul than you know. Something happened between us... twice."

Her face fell, eyes widening in shock and disbelief. "What are you saying, Louis? Just say it."

He swallowed hard, feeling the weight of his words. "Remember that night we went to First Ed before lockdown?" He hesitated, bracing himself. "That night, in the toilets... Paul kissed me."

Her mouth dropped open; her expression frozen in shock. "You're serious?"

Louis nodded, feeling the crushing weight between them. "I thought it was a one-time mistake. Afterwards, we didn't talk for months. But then, at the afters last week... it happened again. We... we hooked up."

A stunned silence settled over them. Her eyes darkened as realisation struck, her face twisted with anger and hurt. "So, my boyfriend—the guy I've been seeing, who I trusted—kissed you months ago, and you didn't think to tell me? And then you went and slept with him?"

"I'm so sorry, Sarah," he said, guilt tearing through him as he saw her pain. "I thought it was a stupid, one-off mistake. That same night, we promised never to let boys come between us. I didn't think Paul and I would ever cross paths again."

She shook her head, fists clenched in anger. "And when I told you I was talking to him, you didn't think that maybe I should know?"

"Back then, I didn't know you two were serious. We'd only been messaging on Instagram—I thought it wouldn't turn into anything." He sighed, voice cracking. "I just felt… alone, and when it happened last week, it was like…"

"Like what?" she snapped, her voice hard and cold. "Like you thought I'd never find out?"

Louis's heart sank as he watched her struggle to hold back tears, anger blazing in her eyes. "I wasn't thinking, Sarah. I just… I wanted to feel wanted."

Her words were venomous, each one a blow. "And you thought it was okay to betray me? To keep this from me?"

He barely managed to look at her. "I didn't want to lose you. I didn't know how to tell you."

"Well, congratulations," she said, her voice trembling as she stepped back. "You've lost me anyway."

"Sarah—please," he whispered, reaching out, but she recoiled, shaking her head in disgust.

"I thought you were my friend, Louis. My best friend." Her voice quivered, laced with hurt. "You've always been jealous. You couldn't stand seeing me happy with someone, so you had to ruin it."

Her words cut deep, leaving him speechless, his throat tight with guilt. She looked at him one last time, her gaze filled with betrayal. "We're done, Louis. Don't ever speak to me again."

She turned and walked away; her shoulders stiff as she disappeared down the path. Louis watched her go, feeling the finality of her departure, each step pulling her further from him and the friendship they'd shared. He tried to call after her, but she didn't look back.

Back home, Louis lay in his bed and stared into the abyss. His phone buzzed with messages from friends asking where he was, but he ignored them all. He couldn't face anyone, replaying his conversation with Sarah in his mind, knowing he'd shattered her trust beyond repair. Alone in his room, he realised he might have lost her and his friends for good.

Earlier that day, Mum had taken Mika to the vet and when she finally returned, she held a small medicine bottle and looked worried. "The vet says Mika has a heart murmur," she explained, her voice strained. "It could be from her collapsed trachea—her heart's working too hard with all that coughing."

Louis spent the evening beside Mika, stroking her fur, feeling a wave of concern for his loyal friend. She settled beside him, and he found comfort in her presence after everything with Sarah.

But just past midnight, Mum gently shook him awake, her face etched with worry. "Louis, Mika's collapsed again. I'm taking her back to the vet."

With his heart pounding, Louis sat up, seeing Mika lying still in his Mum's arms, barely moving. He knelt beside her, his throat tight as he stroked her fur. "Hey, Mika, it's me," he whispered, his voice breaking. Her ears flicked faintly, and he managed a small, tearful smile. "You've been the best dog in the world, you know that?"

Mika's eyes opened a little, meeting his gaze, and he fought back tears. "Remember how you'd follow me everywhere? Always looking out for me." He smiled softly, a bittersweet memory flashing in his mind. "And that Pluto toy—you dragged it around even though it was twice your size. You were like a tiny warrior."

Mum's eyes glistened with tears as she gave him a comforting pat on the shoulder. Leaning in closer, he pressed his forehead gently to Mika's. "I'm going to miss you so much," he whispered. "You are my best friend, Mika. I love you more than anything."

126

With a final, shaky breath, he gave her one last stroke, feeling the warmth of her fur. "You've always been there for me through everything… I'll never forget that." He forced a smile through his tears. "Go be free, okay? I'll carry you with me."

Louis watched from the doorway as Mum cradled Mika and carried her to the car, the weight of goodbye settling heavily on his heart.

When morning came, Mum returned alone, her expression confirming what he'd feared. She sat beside him, her eyes full of sorrow. "Mika's gone, Lou."

Louis broke down, tears flowing as Mum hugged him. They spent the day together on the couch, sharing memories of Mika, laughing through their tears as they remembered her small but fearless spirit—how she'd dive into the waves at the beach, paws splashing, utterly unafraid.

Their memories were bittersweet, each story a tribute to Mika's boundless loyalty and love. Though the loss was painful, Louis knew Mika's memory would stay with them always, a reminder of the joy and comfort she'd brought into their lives.

The days after Mika's passing blended into a fog of grief and loneliness that Louis couldn't shake. News of the new lockdown felt like a final, crushing blow, sealing him in more profound isolation than before. Without Mika, the house felt hollow, and the comforting sounds of her soft padding and jingling collar were now an aching absence.

Mum had tried to reach out, but she was grieving, too. Their conversations dwindled into strained silences, leaving Louis to face his sorrow alone. Once, he'd been surrounded by friends, always a message or call away. Now, his phone was quiet; the silence spoke volumes. It was as if he'd disappeared from everyone's thoughts.

He drifted through the days like a ghost, lost in memories and struggling to find purpose. His usual routines slipped away; meals went uneaten, cold tea sat abandoned, and even the simplest tasks felt overwhelming. It was easier to stay in bed, scrolling through old photos and reliving happier memories. Every laugh, every shared joke with Sarah felt like a life he barely recognised.

One grey afternoon, he forced himself outside, slipping on a hoodie and heading to the park. He walked the paths he and Mika used to roam, her playful barks and nudges haunting him with every step. Watching other families with their dogs made him heartache, and he returned home before the sadness overwhelmed him.

That evening, as he lay in bed, the weight of everything pressed down like a storm cloud he couldn't escape. He thought of reaching out to someone but doubted it would help. Sarah's words from their last argument echoed in his mind, sharp and unforgiving.

Maybe he deserved this loneliness. Perhaps it was his fault.

The following day, he saw a post from Megan, an old college friend, celebrating her acceptance into a journalism course—the same dream he once had. Memories of his article on Nicholas Briggs came flooding back, a reminder of a time when he felt driven and believed in a future filled with possibilities. Now, that version of himself felt like a stranger, replaced by someone he barely recognised.

Mum noticed his withdrawal at once. She had seen him struggle before, but this was different, a sadness she couldn't reach. She tried to pull him out of it, suggesting they cook together or watch a new show, but he brushed her off with little more than a shrug.

One day, she knocked gently on his door and sat beside him on his bed. "Louis," she said softly, "I know things have been hard since Mika... and with the lockdown." Her voice was warm, but he barely looked up from his phone. "Maybe talking to someone would help?"

"I'm fine, Mum," he muttered. "Just tired."

She sighed, not pushing but not giving up, either. "You know you don't have to go through this alone."

But as soon as she left, he let himself slip back into the silence.

As December crept closer, Louis's Mum held onto a glimmer of hope, mentioning Christmas with careful optimism. She started decorating, lighting and ornaments in a quiet attempt to revive their holiday traditions, hoping it might lift his spirits. However, for Louis, each decoration only highlighted the emptiness in their home.

He spent Christmas Eve lost in memories, the warmth of past celebrations now a distant echo. They exchanged gifts in a hushed, obligatory way, and after a quick call with Gran, Mum went to bed early. Left alone in the glow of the Christmas tree, he scrolled through Instagram, hoping to find something comforting.

Instead, he stumbled on a photo of Sarah and Paul, smiling in matching Christmas pyjamas by a brightly lit tree. Her caption read, **"Christmas Eve with my favourite person #grateful."** A sharp and undeniable pang of betrayal struck him. Sarah's smile was as bright as he remembered, but seeing Paul beside her, carefree and content, made Louis's heart sink.

He'd thought their friendship would withstand anything, that she'd see through whatever Paul had told her. But here she was, celebrating with him as if Louis's pain didn't matter. He considered reaching out and sending her a message, but he knew it was useless. She'd made her choice, and he was left to face the emptiness alone.

Closing Instagram, he set his phone down and stared at the Christmas lights, their soft glow only amplifying the silence around him. The loneliness was thick and suffocating as if he were watching the world move on without him, one Christmas light at a time.

New Year's Eve had been a quiet affair, a stark contrast to the previous year's celebration at Carly's house, where laughter and sneaky sips from the drinks cabinet had made the night feel electric with possibility. Now, he found himself sitting on the couch next to his Mum, the distant sound of fireworks a reminder of the year that had quietly slipped away.

His 19th birthday followed, passing as just another day. Mum bought him a small gift, and they had dinner, but it felt routine, lacking the warmth of his last birthday celebration with Carly. Back then, he'd been surprised with a cake at TGI Fridays and shared late-night conversations with Clyde. Now, all he had was the echo of those memories, fading a little more each day.

As January stretched on, Louis felt himself slipping deeper into a heavy numbness, the days blending in an endless cycle of grey mornings and restless nights. His daily routines eroded into nothing; eating became something he did out of habit rather than hunger, and his walks stopped altogether. Each step outside reminded him of Mika, her absence lingering as a dull ache. So, he stayed indoors, scrolling endlessly through his phone, sleeping to pass the time, barely aware of the world around him.

His appearance began to change, with his weight slowly creeping up, a reminder of all the days spent lost in bed,

131

mindlessly snacking. His hair grew out, unruly and unkempt, but he didn't care enough to cut it. The sight of himself in the mirror felt like a reflection of how far he'd drifted, a reminder of the person he no longer thought he was. His Mum and Gran grew increasingly worried, his Gran dropped off his favourite meals, and Mum left pamphlets for mental health support around the house. Despite their gentle attempts, Louis brushed off their efforts, too withdrawn to let anyone in.

One evening, his Gran -who was in his 'COVID social bubble' - visited for dinner and sat across from him at the kitchen table, her hand resting over his in a gentle but firm grasp. "Louis, sweetheart, I know it's been a hard time... with Mika and everything else," she said softly. "But you don't have to go through this alone."

Louis looked down, avoiding her gaze. "I'm fine, Gran. I... need some time."

Her grip tightened, concern filling her eyes. "You've been saying that for months, love. Please, maybe it would help to talk to someone?"

He shook his head, convinced no one could understand his weight and the unshakeable sense of emptiness. She eventually let it go, but the sadness in her eyes lingered, a silent plea he couldn't bring himself to acknowledge.

The days continued to drift by each one, marked by a growing sense of isolation. Late at night, he would scroll through social media, torturing himself with glimpses of friends moving forward with their lives, wondering what they'd think if they saw him now, so lost and heavy with grief.

Then, one morning in March, he woke to his phone vibrating under his pillow. Groggy, he answered, his voice hoarse from disuse. The name on the screen made his breath catch—his Dad. They hadn't spoken in years, and now, after so much silence, Louis felt a glimmer of something he hadn't felt in months. Maybe this was a turning point.

"Louis, it's about my Mum. It's about your Gran." His Dad's words pierced the quiet, his voice low and unsteady.

For a brief, unsteady second, Louis's heart lifted. This is it; he thought. They're finally letting more people visit her. She's not alone anymore. This is the start of things getting better. He sat up straighter, his chest tightening with unexpected anticipation. Maybe things were starting to shift. Perhaps it wasn't all lost.

But then his Dad's voice broke through the quiet again, this time softer, quieter, as if it had to force its way through the weight of the words he was about to say.

"Louis. Your Gran passed away last night."

The words crashed over him like a tidal wave, their weight settling in his chest as he struggled to understand. His Gran, gone? Louis could not remember the last time he had seen his other Gran. Was it months? Years? The grief felt too immense, too surreal to process. He barely registered the rest of the conversation, his Dad's voice distant and muted. When the call ended, he was left holding the phone, staring blankly, the reality of his loss sinking in slowly, numbly.

In the days that followed, Louis drifted through life in a world of his own. Mum stayed close, trying to support him, but it felt like he'd built a wall too high for her to reach over. The thought of his Gran, now just a memory, weighed him further. Every regret, every missed moment haunted him. He barely left his room, scrolling through old photos late into the night, crying silently at the memories of a life that felt so far away now.

One night, as dawn began to break, he found himself wandering downstairs, where his Mum was sitting quietly in the soft glow of the early morning. She looked up, surprise and relief flashing in her tired eyes.

"Mum," he whispered, his voice barely audible. "I... I think I'm ready to get help."

She paused, her eyes searching his face, then softened into a gentle smile as she took his hand. "I'm so proud of you, Louis," she said, her voice thick with emotion.

That small step, calling the doctor, felt like a monumental leap. The doctor's kind words and offer of medication gave him a fragile sense of hope. He sat back, heart racing but lighter, the beginnings of something unfamiliar stirring inside him.

But even as he took this step toward healing, another weight loomed—the funeral and the thought of facing his Dad and brothers after so many years apart. His chest tightened at the thought, and he turned to his Mum, his voice a whisper. "I don't think I can go... I'm not ready."

She nodded; her eyes filled with understanding. "You don't have to, Louis. This is about you and what you need right now."

Louis felt a sense of relief settles over him. The decision to skip the funeral was a minor release from the pressure he'd felt. He would take it daily, one small step at a time. And that felt like enough for the first time in a long while.

CHAPTER NINE
FADED HORIZONS

Louis shook out the pills from the small bottle, feeling the weight of recent weeks begin to ease as he took his medication with renewed commitment. His Mum gave him an encouraging nod as he finished, offering him a comforting smile. Just a few weeks ago, he had felt so distant, unable to attend his other Gran's funeral due to the weight of his struggles. Instead, he and his Mum had held a quiet day of remembrance at home. They shared stories, played her favourite songs, and kept her memory alive, honouring the woman who had been such a significant part of his childhood.

That day reminded Louis how much he needed his Mum's support. Since then, they've developed a new morning routine together, starting their days with a walk around the neighbourhood. Their talks during these walks became a grounding point for him. She shared stories about her memories with her ex-mother-in-law, laughing over the quirks that made her who she was.

One late spring morning, they wandered past a small park, his Mum's arm linked through his when she looked up at him, her eyes soft with hope. "You know, things are finally getting better, love," she said. "I think your Gran would be so proud of you."

Louis nodded, feeling her words sink in. "Yeah, it's starting to feel like things might be okay."

She smiled, squeezing his arm. "I think she would have loved seeing you happy and moving forward."

They continued in silence, but the warmth of her words stayed with him, easing the ache of loss and rekindling his sense of purpose.

In the week that followed, Louis found a new spark of joy in something he'd loved for years: Doctor Who. The new season had just begun, and Jodie Whittaker's return as the Doctor was precisely what he needed to feel inspired again. Watching her travel through alien worlds, facing impossible challenges, reminded him how much he missed writing. So, after the first episode, he decided to review it on his blog. Writing his thoughts felt like rediscovering a piece of himself, and the response from readers was encouraging. They left excitement-filled comments, sharing their theories and favourite scenes.

Week after week, Louis posted his reviews, slowly rebuilding his writing confidence. Each post brought back more of his old passion, making him feel like he was connecting with others again.

As summer unfolded and lockdown restrictions eased, Louis felt a pull toward reclaiming a bit of normalcy. His first stop was the barbershop. Sitting in the familiar worn leather chair, he told the stylist, "Let's make it fresh, yeah? A clean start." Watching his reflection in the mirror as the stylist trimmed away the overgrown strands, he felt lighter. He barely recognised himself at first, but he liked what he saw.

Fresh from the barbershop, he decided to visit his other Gran. He hadn't seen her in person for a while, and the thought of catching up with her brought a rush of warmth. She was thrilled when he called, and within an hour, he was sitting in her cosy living room, sipping tea as she looked at him with pride.

"You look like a young man on a mission," she said, her eyes twinkling.

He chuckled, feeling a bit embarrassed. "I guess I'm just trying to get back on track."

She nodded knowingly. "And what's next for you? Are you still thinking about that journalism course?"

Louis shrugged. "Maybe. It feels far away right now."

"Even so, it wouldn't hurt to start thinking about it," she said gently. "And in the meantime, maybe a part-time job would be a good step forward."

Her advice stayed with him long after he left her house. The idea of a job—something steady to ground him—felt right.

Later that night, he found himself scrolling through local job listings. One posting for a cashier at the fish and chip shop caught his eye. It was familiar, and he imagined what it would be like to work in a place he'd visited so often. Without second-guessing, he applied, updating his CV and hitting send.

That same evening, he received an invitation for an interview the next day. The thought made his heart race, a mix of nerves and excitement.

On the morning of the interview, he picked out a shirt, ensured his hair was brushed, and arrived just in time. The manager, a friendly woman with a warm but no-nonsense manner, asked about his interests and why he wanted the job. He told her about his blog and his love for storytelling, explaining that he hoped to study journalism one day. She seemed impressed by his sincerity.

"Well, we could use someone with your attitude here, Louis. You've got the job if you're interested."

Louis left the shop feeling more grounded than he had in a long time. It was just a job, but it felt like so much more—a small but significant step forward.

Over the next few weeks, he settled into his new routine. Working at the chip shop kept him busy, and though the hours were long, he found comfort in the familiarity of it. There was something satisfying about serving regular customers, learning the rhythms of the place, and earning his pay. On his days off, he returned to his Doctor Who reviews with renewed energy, feeling his confidence as a writer grow with each post.

Louis became friendly with Stephanie and Rebecca, two of his new colleagues at work. Stephanie's infectious laugh and vibrant personality made her easy to talk to. Rebecca, a bit more reserved but just as kind, was always interested in how his writing was going. Their shared shifts became a source of comfort, and before long, they were spending time together outside of work as well. They would grab a coffee after shifts or swap stories about their favourite TV shows.

Louis couldn't help but remember his Gran's words: *"Keep moving forward."* With the support of his family, his growing confidence as a writer, and the companionship of his work friends, he felt ready to begin piecing together a future of his own.

By the time the following Christmas came, things had changed.

Spending the holiday with Mum and Gran under the same roof filled Louis with quiet excitement. The Christmas decorations twinkled softly in the corners of the living room, casting a warm glow that made the house feel alive in a way it hadn't in years. Louis sat on the couch, his eyes drifting to the flickering lights of the tree. The weight of the past year still lingered, but a flicker of hope began to stir beneath it—small but undeniably there.

Just past noon on Christmas Day, Mum called him with a playful smile. "I've got something for you, Lou," she said, her voice filled with expectancy.

Louis blinked; his curiosity piqued. She handed him a small, gift-wrapped box. Inside, he found a shiny collar and a tiny bone-shaped tag attached to a keyring. Puzzled, he raised an eyebrow.

"Go to the kitchen," his Mum urged.

Louis stood, walking to the kitchen door. There, on the floor, sat a small black-and-gold chihuahua puppy, her tiny tail wagging with excitement.

Lottie.

The little dog bounded toward him, slipping on the floor as she leapt into his arms. Louis laughed, something he hadn't done in a long time, and cradled her to his chest. For the first time in ages, he felt something other than sadness.

"You got me a puppy?" he asked, his voice full of disbelief.

His Mum smiled. "I thought she could help, Lou. I know it's been tough."

Louis looked at his Gran, who watched them with a soft smile, her presence calming. Lottie reminded him that sometimes, it was the tiny things that could make an enormous difference. The unconditional love of a pet, the way she nuzzled against him, was a small but comforting step forward.

As the three of them—Louis, Mum, and Gran—spent the rest of the day together, Lottie nestled between them, he allowed himself to feel something he hadn't in a long time: hope. It wasn't blinding or overwhelming but flickered softly, small and steady.

Over the following weeks, that hope grew alongside small steps forward. Louis woke up each day with more energy, his routine slowly shaping itself around the support of those he loved. But with his birthday approaching, a familiar restlessness stirred. Something about turning twenty made him crave change, to feel more like himself again. Maybe a night out would remind him of who he used to be, of the life he'd put on hold.

Turning twenty felt like a milestone for Louis.

He felt like the day should be memorable, even if the weight of the past couple of years still hung around him like a shadow. Stephanie and Rebecca had been insistent on going out, and though he wasn't sure if he was ready, part of him craved some normalcy—a night out, just like old times.

The pubs were busy that night, buzzing with energy. Louis tried to push aside the knot in his stomach, the uncomfortable reminder that he hadn't seen many of his old friends in a long time. But tonight, it was just about fun—a distraction.

Inside First Edition, the familiar lights and noise hit him like a punch to the gut. The laughter, music, and clinking of glasses all felt like a distant memory. People surrounded him, but something about the crowd made him feel more alone than ever. It wasn't the company; the spaces between them and the gaps in conversation reminded him of everything he had lost.

Rebecca's voice cut through his thoughts. "You good, Louis?"

He nodded, plastering on a smile. "Yeah, just... a lot on my mind."

Stephanie raised an eyebrow, her face lighting up with concern. "Don't let it ruin your night, okay? It's your birthday. Let's have fun. You deserve it."

Louis swallowed, nodding again. He had to try. This night could be an escape, even if it didn't feel like it. He reached for his drink, the cold glass almost a lifeline, a way to dull the ache that had started to creep in.

As the hours passed, the drinks kept coming. Each one was a little more liberating, a little less tethered to the life he'd been struggling to live. They went to a new nightclub – The Garage, the second stop on their night out. The place was dim, the music louder, the crowd livelier. He could feel the pulse of the bass vibrating in his chest, and for a moment, it felt like everything else—the grief, the loss, the regrets—was just background noise.

By the time they finally settled into a corner booth, Louis had lost track of how many drinks he'd had. The world around him had blurred, and he felt lighter as if the heaviness he'd been carrying was slowly being lifted. But the more the night went on, the more he could hear the whispers of his old life, the people he no longer saw, the way things used to be before everything started to fall apart.

Stephanie and Rebecca were chatting, laughing about something he wasn't paying attention to. His eyes drifted over the room, and suddenly, he saw Sarah, Paul, Carly, Lauren, and Karen.

Everything felt too familiar. People he used to laugh with, people who had slipped away as his world crumbled. It all felt too much. The weight of it all—his failed relationships, the friendships he had let fade, the emptiness he'd been trying to fill—flooded him in a rush.

The grief hit him like a wave, a sharp, overwhelming emotion that he couldn't outrun. At that moment, Louis didn't care about hiding it anymore. The tears came before he could stop them, hot and unrelenting, trickling down his cheeks as the music throbbed around him. He didn't know if anyone noticed or if they even cared, but it didn't matter.

"Louis?" Rebecca's voice was gentle, but it barely reached him. She was still talking, but he couldn't hear her words over the noise in his head.

Before he could say anything, he felt the familiar pull to disappear—to slip away, to hide from the mess he had become. "I need to go," he mumbled, standing up abruptly. The room spun as he tried to walk, but everything was off-balance. The door felt so far away, the night stretching out before him like a tunnel with no exit.

Stephanie called after him, but he didn't stop. He didn't need anyone's pity. He just needed to get away.

The cold air hit him as he stumbled outside, his mind still whirling, his stomach turning. He found a bench, sat down, and let his head fall into his hands. The silence felt deafening after the bar's noise, but even it couldn't drown out the spiralling thoughts in his mind. He couldn't help but think of everything he had lost— the friends who had faded from his life, the hopes and dreams that had slipped away with each passing day.

And then, the familiar voice in his head whispered: *You don't need the medication anymore. You're fine. You're doing fine.*

The lie felt so easy, so simple to believe. He'd been on the medication for so long, but it didn't seem to do much anymore. He didn't need it, did he? He'd made it this far, hadn't he? But in his mind, he knew it wasn't true. He only told himself to avoid confrontations with his Mum and Gran. It was easier this way. It's more straightforward to hide it. Easier to pretend.

When he finally made his way home later that night, the alcohol still clouding his senses, the reality of what had happened hit him. His Mum's worried face flashed in his mind, the way she always seemed to know when something was off. The way she would ask how he was feeling if he was still taking his pills. But tonight, he hadn't been honest with her. He couldn't remember the last time he'd been candid with anyone.

He staggered through the door and walked straight into the kitchen. Mum was busy in the living room, watching TV, her back turned. He reached for the small bottle of medication on the counter, where he'd left it earlier in the day. He opened it, shook the last few pills into his palm, and stared at them for a long moment.

He wasn't sure why he even bothered to pick them up anymore. He didn't need them. He hadn't taken them in days, had he? Maybe a week? The thought of them—those little pills that had been a part of his routine for so long—felt like an inconvenience now. He felt better without them. Maybe he didn't need to keep pretending.

With a heavy sigh, he slipped them into his pocket and went upstairs to his bedroom. He opened the drawer, where he kept a few personal things tucked away, and dropped the pills inside, out of sight. The drawer shut with a soft click. It felt like a small victory.

But as he sat on his bed, the weight of his thoughts pressed down on him. What was he doing? He lied to everyone—his Mum, Gran, and even himself. The truth was, he didn't feel better. He felt worse. But admitting that felt like a defeat. And he wasn't sure if he was ready to face it.

As he lay down, the room's quiet settled around him, and he tried to sleep, but the guilt lingered. There was no escaping the growing realisation that he had made a bad choice by not taking his pills—and now, he didn't know how to turn back.

The following day, Louis woke to his Mum calling up the stairs. He rubbed his eyes, groggy from the night before, and knew the day ahead would be another step into the mess he was trying to avoid. But as he pulled himself out of bed, he couldn't ignore the weight in his chest—the nagging sense that he was slowly slipping into a depressive state again.

The months went on, and Louis's mental health continued to deteriorate. The grief, isolation, and uncertainty about his future pushed him deeper into old habits. On weekends, he would end up at parties, surrounded by laughter and music that only seemed to amplify his sense of detachment. It wasn't the socialising he sought—it was the escape. The drugs, the alcohol, the numbness. It was easier than confronting the ache inside. But the more he sought it, the less the high seemed to help. Each weekend, he grew more reliant on substances, each high feeling like a reprieve from the weight of everything. The cycle repeated: the highs became shorter, the lows more bottomless, and his stability eroded.

Once a grounding force, his job at the fish and chip shop began to feel like another distraction—a place to hide from himself. The steady routine of serving customers and the simple task of frying fish and chips allowed him to exist without genuinely engaging with his thoughts. But even that comfort began to lose its appeal. His passion for writing, which had once been a source of solace and purpose, slipped further away. He could no longer bring himself to write the Doctor Who reviews that had once ignited a spark in him. Instead, he buried his time and energy in work and fleeting nights out, using the noise and chaos as a shield against the reality of his inner turmoil.

Louis's Mum and Gran noticed the shift in him. His Mum, significantly, was growing more concerned. She had hoped that time and his job would help Louis find his way, but she could see how much he was retreating. The spark he once had for his writing and dreams was fading.

One evening, when Louis sat at the kitchen table with a glass of water in front of him, she asked him directly.

"Lou, do you still want to go back to college? You've told me before that you wanted to study journalism, but now… it's like you don't even think about it anymore."

Louis shifted uncomfortably in his chair, avoiding her gaze. "I don't know. It feels too far away right now. I need another year to figure things out."

His Mum didn't push. She nodded, but the worry in her eyes was unmistakable.

Louis had stopped taking his medication a few weeks earlier. It wasn't a conscious decision at first; it happened gradually. He had felt better—at least, he thought he had—and the pills seemed less necessary. He kept picking them up, though, for appearances. He didn't want to raise any suspicions with Mum, so he quietly stashed them in his bedroom drawers, out of sight, out of mind. The act of taking the pills felt like a reminder of a time he wanted to move past. The numbness from the drugs had replaced the temporary relief the medication once gave him, and in his mind, that was enough.

But deep down, he knew it wasn't. He knew that running from his emotions, from the pain, wasn't going to fix anything. Yet he didn't know where to go next. His dreams of being a journalist felt further out of reach than ever, and the sense of direction he once had seemed to be slipping away.

An evening that weekend, after Louis had come home late, his Mum couldn't hold it in any longer. She stood in the doorway of his room, arms crossed, her expression a mix of concern and frustration.

"You need to stop this, Louis," she said, her voice firm but tinged with worry. "You've been out every weekend for weeks, and I barely see you during the week. What happened to the boy who used to want to be a journalist? You had dreams, Lou. You were going to make something of yourself."

Louis froze, the weight of her words sinking in. He didn't want to hear it, not now. He was tired of the expectations, trying to meet them, and feeling like he was constantly disappointing her. So, he shrugged it off, trying to act nonchalant.

"I'm just taking a break, Mum. It's fine. I'll figure it out," he said, but his tone was defensive, almost dismissive.

Her face softened, but there was a sharp edge to her words. "It's not fine, Louis. You're running from everything, and I'm tired of pretending I don't see it. You used to talk about your future like it was right before you, but now? You don't even seem to care. I'm not asking you to have it all figured out, but I am asking you to think about where you're headed."

Louis felt a lump form in his throat. He wanted to argue, to shout that she didn't understand, that she couldn't know what he was going through. But instead, he crossed his arms and looked away, feeling the tension between them stretch even further. He hated this conversation, hated how it made him feel small like he was letting everyone down.

"I don't need you to lecture me," he muttered. "I'm fine."

His Mum shook her head, her eyes welling up with tears. "I'm not lecturing you, Louis. I'm just... I'm just worried. You have so much potential, and I can't watch you throw it away. You've always had big dreams. Could you not give up on them now? Not like this."

The words stung more than Louis expected, and he felt a knot of guilt twist in his stomach. But instead of confronting those feelings, he lashed out defensively. "I'm not giving up on anything, Mum. You're the one who keeps pushing me. Maybe I don't want to go back to college. Maybe I don't care about journalism anymore."

The silence between them was heavy, the unspoken truth hanging like a cloud that neither could disperse. Louis's Mum turned and left his room without another word, her heart heavy with disappointment.

Louis sat there for a long time after, staring at the wall. Her words echoed in his mind, gnawing at him. But the more he thought about it, the more he wanted to retreat further into the life he'd built and the distractions he had created. His Mum didn't understand. She didn't see the weight he carried, the way his dreams felt like they were slipping through his fingers. It was easier to push her away than face the painful truth about himself—the fear, the uncertainty, the guilt.

But in his heart, he knew it wasn't just his Mum he was distancing himself from. It was everything he used to care about. And that scared him more than anything.

Louis sat in bed long after his Mum's footsteps faded down the hallway. The silence in his room felt suffocating, as though the walls were pressing in on him. He could still feel the sting of her words, the disappointment in her eyes. You've got so much potential, she'd said. But what if he didn't? What if, deep down, he had nothing left to give? His mind repeated their conversation, the guilt gnawing at him, twisting in his stomach.

His gaze drifted toward the old shoebox under his bed—untouched for months, maybe longer. It was the box that held everything he used to care about: old photos, ticket stubs, scraps of paper filled with ideas for stories he'd never written, dreams he no longer had the strength to chase. He used to look at those things and feel alive and inspired. Now, they just reminded him of how far he'd fallen.

With a shaky breath, he slid out from under the covers, the cold air hitting his skin like a shock. The box felt heavy in his hands, the weight of everything it represented pressing down on him. He sat back on his bed and opened it slowly as though afraid to disturb what was left inside.

The first thing he pulled out was a photo—him, much younger, standing with his Dad at a Glasgow police box. A distant memory; frozen in time, when he still believed he had a future, when he still had hope. The photo's edges were slightly worn but still held that spark. He felt the tears well up in his eyes before he even realised it. How had he gone from that bright-eyed boy full of possibilities to this broken version of himself?

He moved through the box, pulling out more reminders—his old journal, some notes from his interview with Nicholas Briggs, a cinema ticket for "Rocketman" he'd seen during his college years. The memories stung. They felt so distant, so unreachable now.

Each item seemed to weigh him down more, a reminder of the life he once had and the person he once was. He closed his eyes, tears slipping down his face as the guilt overwhelmed him. *What happened to me?* He thought. *What happened to my dreams?*

He couldn't stop the tears now. They came in heavy, unstoppable waves. The pain felt too much to bear, and at that moment, he didn't know how to escape it. He opened his bedside drawer, pulling out a small tub filled with pills he hadn't taken. He had told himself he wouldn't go back to them, that he could get better on his own, that he didn't need the pills anymore. But tonight, everything felt different. Tonight, he felt like he had nothing left.

With trembling hands, he took the tub and poured out the pills, watching them spill across the sheets of his bed. He wasn't sure how many would make it stop; how many it would take for him to numb the pain. But tonight, he didn't want to take chances.

He began to split the pills into piles, ten at a time. Each pile felt like a decision, a choice to escape the weight of life. The weight of *HIS* life. His heart pounded in his chest, and his vision blurred from the tears. But still, he kept going, counting out piles of pills. Ten pills in one pile. Ten more in the next. The piles grew more extensive, a reflection of the heaviness inside him.

When he had enough, he stared down at them, the small pills sitting there like a final answer, like the only way out. He could feel the pressure building, the crushing weight of everything that had gone wrong, everything that had slipped through his fingers. He reached for the first pile, his hand shaking uncontrollably, and swallowed the pills one by one—ten, then ten more, and again. The bitter taste filled his mouth, but he didn't care.

Maybe this will make it stop, he thought.

His vision began to blur, and his body grew heavy. He lay back on the bed, staring at the ceiling, feeling his pulse slow and his thoughts drifting in and out of focus. The world seemed so far away that it was happening to someone else. He welcomed the numbness, the quiet.

But as the darkness crept in, a small part of him—a part he barely recognised—whispered something he couldn't ignore. *What if it's not too late?*

The thought was fleeting, lost in the haze, but for a minute, it was enough to make him pause.

He closed his eyes, unsure if he was making a choice or just letting go. The silence in the room enveloped him, but he wasn't sure if he was fading out or had one last chance to fight.

Louis woke up with a throbbing headache that seemed to pulse in time, with the light slipping through his curtains. His head pounded as he sat up, groggy and nauseated. He checked his phone — half past noon. He couldn't remember the last time he'd slept in this late. He shut his eyes again, willing the room to stop spinning.

He spent the entire morning in bed, half-drifting between thoughts and uneasy sleep, trying to ignore the sense of heaviness pressing down on his chest. The events of the previous night replayed in his mind: his Mum's worried tone, taking all those pills. He felt like he'd let her down like he'd let himself down. He couldn't keep dragging her through the confusion and sadness he hadn't yet figured out for himself. But where to even begin?

As the day stretched on, he stayed in his room, avoiding his Mum, not wanting to deal with her worried looks or questions. He tried to eat but couldn't manage more than a few bites. Instead, he lay back on his bed, staring at the ceiling, mulling over his options. He knew he couldn't stay here like this forever, waiting for change. There had been a time when he'd felt alive, independent, ready to chase down life — like back in college, when he'd stayed up late with friends, eager for every new day. Or that trip to London, exploring the city, meeting new people, and feeling a sense of purpose with each step he took. He missed that version of himself.

He was twenty now, but he felt smaller, tied down in a way that left him no room to breathe. His Mum and Gran tried to help, but their care felt like a reminder of how much he was falling short. He knew they only worried because they loved him, but he needed to find his way. He needed space to confront whatever he was running from.

That's when the thought finally became clear and insistent: He needed to move out. Maybe getting his place would be the first step in figuring things out. A new place could allow him to grow on his terms. He could manage it — or at least, he had to try. And as much as he hated the idea of leaving his Mum and Lottie, he could not shake the feeling that this was what he needed to feel like himself again.

By evening, he felt more settled in his decision. He would look for a flat nearby — close enough to visit his family but far enough to give himself the distance to heal.

CHAPTER TEN
A NEW HOME, A NEW LOUIS

The early spring sunlight streamed through the bedroom window as Louis lifted a cardboard box, its contents rattling slightly. He placed it on his bed, which was already stripped down to the mattress. Outside, the streets were alive with people shaking off the weight of winter, but inside, he was packing away reminders of the past year—the one he was trying so hard to leave behind.

His Mum was folding up the last of his clothes, Lottie curled beside her on the bed, her tiny body pressed against his Mum's side...

"This brings back memories, doesn't it?" Mum smiled, pulling a pair of old high-tops from one of the boxes. "Remember these? You practically wore them out that summer."

Louis grinned, taking the shoes from her hands. "How could I forget? I must've walked miles in these, even after the soles started falling apart."

They laughed, letting a wave of nostalgia wash over them, the tension in the air giving way to warmth. Lottie perked up as if sensing their laughter and leaned her head on Louis's leg, her dark eyes watching him closely.

As they packed, little mementoes of Louis's childhood emerged—old birthday cards, a half-written journal from his college days, and his first collection of books on journalism. Holding them now, they felt like artefacts from another lifetime. Louis's Mum picked up a LEGO figure he'd given her before his trip to London. She traced her fingers over it, smiling softly.

"You know," she said, her voice shaky, "maybe this is what you need. Maybe moving out could be the making of you. You'll have space to breathe, to... find that bright-eyed boy who used to have dreams as big as the world."

Louis swallowed, the lump in his throat rising. "I hope so, Mum. I know I've... drifted. I want to get back to him, too."

Mum nodded, blinking a few times before pulling him into a tight hug. "I'll miss you so much, Louis. It won't be the same even if you're just ten minutes down the road. You'll always be my little boy."

A silence hung between them, words heavy with love and concern left unspoken. Lottie let out a little whine, shifting against Louis, as if she, too, sensed the change that was coming.

Once everything was packed, they loaded the car with the last of his belongings. The drive to his new flat in town was quiet, the weight of the moment settling over them. Louis gazed out the window, taking in the passing streets, knowing they were close to home but that everything was about to feel different.

The flat was modest, a one-bedroom in a slightly worn complex just minutes from the centre of town. It had a surprisingly spacious living room; made brighter by the fresh coat of white paint he'd put on the walls. They'd already moved in the essentials—a bed, a grey couch from Facebook Marketplace, and a small table and chairs for his kitchen. It was basic, but as Louis looked around, he felt an unexpected rush of pride. This was his.

"This is perfect, Louis," Mum said, placing a few pillows on the couch. "It's got character. I can see you making a real home here."

Louis nodded, half-smiling. "Yeah, it's cosy. I think I'll like it."

They looked around together, silently taking in the space that would now be his. Lottie trotted around, sniffing corners and investigating, her little paws clicking on the floor. She looked up at him expectantly, and Louis knelt to scratch her ears. "Guess you're sticking with Mum, Lottie. My hours are all over the place at the shop, and I don't want you to be alone too much."

Lottie gave a small bark, almost as if she understood. His Mum stroked the dog's back, nodding in agreement. "She'll be fine with me. Besides, now I'll have a little piece of you with me all the time." Her eyes glistened as she glanced away, taking in the flat one last time. "Just don't forget to visit us. It's still your home, too."

Louis hugged her, longer this time, feeling her warmth and the reassurance of her presence. He didn't want to let go but knew he had to.

"I love you, Mum," he said softly. "Thank you. For... everything."

"Love you too, Louis. And I'll always be here. Remember that."

As the door clicked shut, Louis stood in his empty flat, a strange mix of excitement and loneliness washing over him. He looked around, hands in his pockets, letting the quiet settle. For the first time, he was completely on his own.

He wandered from room to room, letting the reality of it sink in. In the small kitchen, the smell of fresh paint lingered. The cabinets were bare except for a couple of mugs and a single chipped bowl he'd found at a charity shop. He chuckled, realising he'd probably need to buy more dishes if he didn't want to be washing this one every meal.

In the living room, sunlight slanted through the window, casting a warm glow over the grey couch they'd hauled in yesterday. He sank down on it, testing the cushions. It wasn't the comfiest thing, but it would do for now. The blank walls and minimal furniture left the place feeling a little like a temporary stay rather than a home, but he knew that would change over time, as he added more of his own touches.

He pulled out his phone, scrolling mindlessly through messages. His friends from the fish and chip shop had sent some jokes and a few good-luck texts, but it was his Mum's last message that he kept re-reading:

I will miss you every day. You know where to find me. Be good to yourself, Louis. I love you more than you'll ever know.

He put the phone down and looked over at the small stack of boxes by the wall, filled with mementoes from his old room. He decided to start unpacking them, thinking it might help him feel a bit more settled. One by one, he pulled things out—a worn paperback of The Hunger Games, a poster he'd kept from his first Radio class, a small picture frame with a faded photo of him and his Mum at Christmas years ago. Each item brought a memory with it, and he found himself smiling as he set them up around the room.

Finally, he picked up a small wooden box his Gran had given him when he'd started college. Inside was a notebook she'd gifted him, with his name embossed in gold letters on the cover, and a pen that hadn't left his side during his early days of studying. He opened the notebook, flipping through blank pages, memories of old dreams stirring inside him. He hadn't written anything meaningful in so long, but seeing it here now, in his own place, a tiny spark of that old drive flared up.

It was strange, the idea of starting fresh. It wasn't like the move would erase everything he'd been through, but maybe, just maybe, it would give him a chance to find a new part of himself. To shake off some of the weight he'd been carrying.

A soft knock on the door broke him from his thoughts. He opened it to find his neighbour from across the hall, a middle-aged woman with greying hair tied back in a neat ponytail. She smiled warmly.

"Hi, I'm Tracy from upstairs," she said, holding a small plate with two brownies wrapped in plastic. "Figured you could use a bit of a welcome. Moving day's always rough."

"Thanks," Louis said, surprised but touched by the gesture. "I'm Louis. Just moved in today."

"Nice to meet you, Louis. It's a good little flat. I've been here about ten years myself, so if you need anything or run into trouble, feel free to give me a knock." She smiled before handing over the brownies. "Good luck with everything."

He thanked her and shut the door, a soft smile lingering on his face as he unwrapped one of the brownies and took a bite. It was warm, gooey, and surprisingly good. It reminded him of home, of simpler times, and it settled something in his chest.

As the sun dipped lower in the sky, Louis walked over to the window, looking out over the small stretch of town. The streets below were quiet, just the distant hum of passing cars. For the first time in a while, he felt a flicker of hope—a tentative sense that maybe this was exactly what he needed.

He sat down on the couch, reached for his notebook, and, with a deep breath, put pen to paper. He didn't know what he was writing or if it even mattered, but it felt right. With each word, a bit of the weight he'd been carrying started to ease, and for the first time in months, he allowed himself to imagine what he might find here in this small flat—his own space, his own life, and maybe, with a little time, his way back to himself.

Louis was settling into bed when his phone buzzed on the nightstand. He reached over, expecting a message from his Mum—she'd promised to check in before bed. But when he unlocked the screen, he saw Sarah's name instead. The message began:

"I saw your Mum's Facebook post, Louis. Congratulations on your own flat!"

He stared at it, his heart catching in his chest. They hadn't spoken in over two years, not since everything had started to fall apart. The next line, though, hit him even harder:

"I know it's been a couple of years, but I'm really sorry, and… you were right about Paul."

Louis blinked, processing. The argument about Paul had driven a wedge between him and his friends, especially Sarah. He'd tried to tell her what he'd seen in Paul, but she hadn't wanted to hear it back then. He hadn't expected to hear this now.

She continued,

"I hope we can bridge the gap. We all miss you."

A photo came through next: Sarah, Karen, and the rest of the old gang, smiling together in Sarah's living room, faces warm and familiar. Seeing them all together again brought back a flood of memories—FaceTime marathons, shared laughs, late-night drives, and the unwavering closeness they'd once had.

He stared at the screen, the image stirring something he hadn't felt in a long time. For the past couple of years, he'd convinced himself he didn't need them, that he was better off without the people who hadn't understood him. But here, alone in his empty flat, he couldn't deny the pang of longing he felt. Despite everything, a part of him had missed them too.

He wasn't sure how to respond. He felt like so much had changed like he'd drifted too far from who he'd been back then. Would he even fit back into their lives, or was it better to keep the distance, to hold on to the person he was trying to become?

But then he remembered his Mum's words from earlier— *"Maybe moving out could be the making of you. Maybe you'll find that bright-eyed boy with dreams again."* Maybe reconnecting with people who'd known that version of him would help him find his way back, even if it took time.

He took a deep breath and started typing.

"Hey, Sarah. Thanks for the message. It's been a long time, but I'd like that. Miss you all too."

He paused, then added,

"Maybe we could catch up sometime."

Before he could overthink it, he hit send.

In the few weeks since he'd moved in, Louis had been busy setting up his place, personalising it bit by bit. A picture from home here, a thrifted wall clock there. He'd even painted a few old frames he found at a charity shop, his collection of small décor slowly coming together. His Gran bought him a microwave that fit perfectly with his black kitchen tiles, a little slice of home every time he reheated leftover meals. Between the bills and decorating, it was a balancing act, but one he felt proud to be handling.

Each visit from Mum or Gran was welcome, bringing warmth and familiarity to his new space. His Gran especially loved popping by to check on his "progress." She'd always arrive with a treat—whether it was homemade scones, a bag of groceries, or the latest housewarming gift. she made him feel like this little flat was just as much her project as his.

After one of her visits, he noticed a voicemail blinking on his phone. It was Sarah, checking in again. He'd been hesitant at first, not quite sure if he wanted to let old friendships back in, but her message sounded genuine, her tone hopeful. They'd exchanged a few messages over the last week, and it felt surprisingly natural. Sarah had even mentioned getting together with the old gang soon, "like the good old days," she'd said, and for the first time, Louis found himself looking forward to the idea.

His evenings were often quiet. While he occasionally ran into Stephanie and Rebecca at work, he hadn't joined them for a night out since that chaotic one a while back. The memory of it, raw and unresolved, lingered. Still, he was content with nights spent on the couch, planning small adjustments to the flat or flipping through the old journal he'd started writing in again.

On a sunny Saturday afternoon, he heard a soft knock on his door. Expecting a delivery, he opened it to find Sarah, a smile brightening her face. She held out a small houseplant, a fern in a quirky ceramic pot.

"For the new flat!" she chirped. "I thought it might add a bit of life here."

Louis couldn't help but laugh as he welcomed her inside, placing the plant on a shelf. It suited the place, brightening up a corner he hadn't quite known how to fill.

They caught up, laughing over old stories, and it felt good, comfortable. Sarah asked about the job, and he shared a few funny stories from the shop. He noticed that, despite the emotional distance created over the last couple of years, the trust and ease he felt with her hadn't disappeared entirely.

Days rolled into weeks, and Louis found himself settling into a rhythm. Work, home, catching up with friends. He wasn't sure when he'd last felt so balanced, even if things were far from perfect. Every small step he took in building this new life felt like a nod to the person he was becoming, someone who didn't just rely on others to feel whole but could stand steady on his own.

One evening, after another long day, Louis flopped onto his couch, breathing in the quiet. His phone buzzed with a text from his Mum.

"I hope you're eating well and taking care. Remember, you'll always have a home with me. Love you xx."

He let himself smile. While parts of him still felt unfinished, like loose threads yet to be tied, he felt something shift—a glimmer of hope that he might be getting somewhere, making a life he could call his own.

That summer came quickly, which caught Louis off guard. He'd spent most of the spring focused on his new flat, turning the blank walls and empty spaces into a reflection of himself. The once-bare walls now displayed thrifted art prints and a gallery of photographs—some of Mika, others from family gatherings or carefree outings with friends. A citrus-scented candle burned on the windowsill, its zesty aroma a subtle reminder of home.

After a long shift at the chip shop, Louis had tossed his uniform into the washing basket and changed into a pair of jeans and a faded T-shirt. As he stood in the middle of his flat, he let out a quiet sigh of satisfaction. The space felt like his—a sanctuary he had carefully pieced together with care and intention.

167

In the kitchen, he arranged a bouquet of white and pink carnations into a ceramic vase. It had been a thoughtful housewarming gift from Sarah, and now it sat proudly on the counter, a small burst of colour against the clean white tiles. Tomorrow would be a big day—he was hosting a dinner party for Sarah, Carly, Lauren, and Karen. It had been years since all five of them had been in the same room together, and as much as Louis was looking forward to it, a nervous knot twisted in his stomach.

It wasn't that he didn't want to see them; he did, desperately. But things had grown messy over time. Life had pulled him away, and in the chaos, he'd drifted from the group that had once been his lifeline.

As he sat at the kitchen table, Louis exhaled deeply. Months earlier, Sarah had reached out to reconnect, her invitation tugging at his guilt and hope in equal measure. He'd hesitated, unsure if the others had outgrown him. But tomorrow, they would all gather again. He wanted it to go well, to feel the way it used to.

That evening the flat buzzed with laughter and conversation. Chinese takeout containers cluttered the table, the air rich with the aroma of sweet and sour sauce. In the living room, dim lamplight cast a cosy glow as a comedy film played softly in the background.

Lauren was curled up in the armchair, her plate of chow Mein balanced on her lap. Across the room, Carly animatedly recounted her recent graduation from her business course.

"I can't believe I'm finally done," Carly exclaimed, raising her glass of white wine. "It feels surreal to have that degree after all those late nights and panic attacks over exams."

"You smashed it, though," Sarah said from the couch, where she and Karen were sharing a blanket. "Meanwhile, I just finished my nursing degree, and let me tell you, I haven't slept properly in months."

Karen nudged her with a grin. "But now you can save lives and sleep—living the dream!"

Their laughter was infectious, the kind that came easily from shared memories and deep-rooted affection. Louis smiled, soaking in the warmth of the night. The tension he'd felt earlier eased, replaced by gratitude for having them here again.

But even as they laughed and reminisced, Louis felt a faint ache of distance. These girls had been his lifeline for years, their late-night lockdown calls and inside jokes were once a constant in his life. Now, the language they spoke felt a little foreign, the familiarity of the past tinged with the sharpness of time apart.

"You've done well for yourself," Carly said, her eyes sweeping across the flat. "It's so... you. Cosy, stylish, just the right amount of quirky."

Louis chuckled, a blush creeping across his cheeks. "Thanks. I'm still figuring things out."

Karen raised an eyebrow playfully. "Aren't we all?"

The evening ended too quickly, the flat falling silent once the goodbyes had been said. Louis lingered in the living room; his gaze drawn to the photos on the wall. They were snapshots of a life he'd almost lost memories of laughter, connection, and belonging. Yet, the feeling of being stuck clung to him, a reminder of how everyone else seemed to be moving forward while he remained in place.

The crisp breeze carried the change into autumn. One Sunday morning, Louis sat at his kitchen table with a steaming mug of hot chocolate. The flat felt too quiet lately, a stillness that gnawed at him since he'd said goodbye to Lottie.

He opened his laptop and began researching small pets— budgies, guinea pigs, hamsters. As he scrolled through rescue listings, a scruffy orange-and-white cat caught his eye. Her bright green eyes seemed to stare straight through the screen.

Later that week, Louis found himself at the shelter, face-to-face with the cat from the listing. She pressed her nose against the glass of her enclosure, her tail flicking with curiosity.

"She's a wee cutie," the shelter worker said, smiling. "Her name's Hope."

Louis crouched to her eye level, his lips quirking into a soft smile. "Hi, Hope," he murmured, lightly tapping the glass. Her raspy meow was immediate and insistent, tugging at his heart.

"She's just over five," the worker added. "Independent but loves attention. Perfect for someone who works during the day but wants a companion."

When Hope finally stepped out of her enclosure, she approached Louis cautiously, brushing against his knee before meeting his gaze expectantly. Her green eyes were warm, filled with a trust that felt like a gift.

At that moment, Louis knew.

The flat transformed with Hope's arrival. She explored every corner with deliberate curiosity, from batting at the fern on the windowsill to claiming her favourite spot on the back of the couch. Over time, they found a rhythm—Hope following Louis as he did housework, her tail flicking with playful energy.

One evening, as Louis sat journaling at the kitchen table, Hope sprawled across his notebook, her green eyes staring up at him expectantly. He laughed, gently moving her to the side.

"You're going to be trouble, aren't you?" he said, scratching behind her ears.

Her purr was immediate and satisfied, filling the room with a comforting hum.

The chill of October settled in, crisp and biting, as Louis walked home from work. The town was alive with Halloween decorations—glowing jack-o'-lanterns on doorsteps, fake cobwebs stretched across fences, and skeletons dangling from

171

windows. A few houses even had motion-activated decorations that cackled or howled as you passed. Louis smirked when one startled a passing dog walker, their Labrador barking indignantly at the mechanical witch.

Inside his flat, Hope was perched on the windowsill, her green eyes watching the street below. She had taken a particular interest in the parade of costumes over the past few days—children in superhero capes, adults in witches' hats, and even the occasional pet in a pumpkin-shaped outfit.

"Bet you'd look adorable in one of those," Louis teased as he set down his bag. Hope flicked her tail, unimpressed.

Louis had always loved Halloween. Growing up, it was one of the few times of the year that felt magical—an evening where the mundane world slipped away, replaced by shadowy figures and flickering lights. His Gran would carve intricate designs into pumpkins while Mum made toffee apples, the sweet smell filling the kitchen.

This year, though, he hadn't planned anything special. He'd considered going out with his work friends—Stephanie had invited him to a costume party—but the idea of loud music and packed rooms didn't appeal to him. Instead, he decided to spend the night at home, keeping things low-key.

As the evening rolled on, Louis pulled out the pumpkin he'd bought earlier in the week. It wasn't much—just a modest-sized squash—but he was determined to carve something decent.

He spread newspaper across the kitchen table and set to work, scooping out the seeds and tracing a simple design.

Hope watched intently from her perch, occasionally swiping at stray bits of pumpkin that rolled her way.

"Not bad, huh?" Louis said, stepping back to admire his handiwork. The face was simple but expressive—two triangular eyes and a toothy grin.

He placed a tea light inside and set the jack-o'-lantern on the windowsill. The warm glow filled the room, casting flickering shadows on the walls. Hope sniffed at the pumpkin before retreating to her favourite spot on the couch.

Later, Louis curled up with a blanket and a mug of hot chocolate, his laptop open to a playlist of classic Halloween movies. He started with Hocus Pocus—a childhood favourite—and followed it with The Nightmare Before Christmas. Hope stretched out beside him, her head resting on his leg.

Every so often, the sound of laughter or footsteps echoed from the street outside. Louis had set out a bowl of sweets for trick-or-treaters, though there hadn't been many so far.

As the night deepened, Louis found himself lost in thought. Halloween had always been about escapism, about stepping into another world for just a little while. This year, it felt different—quieter, but not in a bad way.

For the first time in years, Louis felt content with the simplicity of the evening. He didn't need the parties or the noise—just the little things: a carved pumpkin, a mug of cocoa, and the quiet companionship of his cat.

When the last movie ended, Louis blew out the candle in the jack-o'-lantern and carried Hope to bed. As he drifted off to sleep, the glow of Halloween lingered in his mind—a reminder that even in the quietest moments, there was still magic to be found.

CHAPTER ELEVEN
TURNING THE PAGE

In a flash of work and playful nights with Hope - December arrived in full, wrapping the town in a chill that Louis both loved and dreaded. The streets were lined with glowing fairy lights, shop windows decked out with wreaths and ribbons, and a faint scent of cinnamon and roasted chestnuts lingered in the air. The holiday season always stirred a mix of emotions for him— warm nostalgia tangled with bittersweet memories.

He pulled his coat tighter as he stepped out of the fish and chip shop, the rush of warmth from the fryer replaced by the icy bite of the evening air. It was Christmas Eve, and the streets were quieter than usual, most people already home wrapping gifts or sipping mulled wine.

By the time Louis reached his flat, he was greeted by a familiar sight: Hope, his mischievous cat, tangled in the garland that had been draped across the mantle just that morning. She blinked up at him, her green eyes innocent despite the mess of red berries and pinecones now scattered across the floor.

"Hope!" Louis groaned, dropping his bag by the door. "I can't leave you alone for five minutes, can I?"

Hope chirped in response, hopping down and weaving around his legs as he picked up the garland. The flat smelled faintly of pine, thanks to the modest artificial tree in the corner.

Its twinkling lights reflected off shiny baubles, and near the top hung a paper snowflake he had made as a child—its slightly crinkled edges a testament to years of care.

He tidied up the garland, draping it back into place, and checked the tree for any signs of Hope's earlier escapades. A small, knitted robin was slightly askew, but otherwise, the decorations had survived.

"All right, you little terror," Louis muttered, scratching behind her ears. "You've had your fun. Let's keep it intact until tomorrow, yeah?"

Christmas morning dawned quietly, the first light filtering through the fairy lights framing the window. Louis stretched, groaning as Hope jumped onto his chest with a soft meow.

"Merry Christmas to you too," he chuckled, setting her down and padding to the kitchen. He set a pot of milk to warm on the hob, stirring in cocoa powder and sugar until the rich scent of hot chocolate filled the air.

As he sipped his drink, a knock at the door startled him. He opened it to find his Gran standing there, bundled in her coat and holding a box of homemade mince pies.

"Gran!" Louis exclaimed, stepping aside to let her in. "What are you doing here? I thought you weren't coming!"

"Did you think I'd let you spend your first Christmas here alone?" she replied with a twinkle in her eye.

Gran wasted no time making herself at home. She cooed over the decorations, particularly the tree, and commented on how cosy the flat felt. Louis could not help but beam under her praise—it had taken weeks to pull everything together, but seeing her smile made it worth it.

By midday, another knock sounded at the door. Louis opened it to find his Mum, arms full of presents and Lottie, her black-and-gold chihuahua, tucked under one arm.

"Surprise!" his Mum chirped, stepping inside. Following her was Fred, her new boyfriend, carrying a bottle of wine and a tin of biscuits.

Louis raised an eyebrow. "Fred, right?"

"Good to finally meet you," Fred said warmly, extending a hand.

Louis hesitated but shook it. He had heard about Fred—how kind he was, how much he made his Mum laugh—but this was the first time they'd met. Still, he couldn't help but feel a little protective.

As the afternoon wore on, Gran had left to visit Louis' cousins in Glasgow. His Mum's boyfriend Fred proved easy company. He helped in the kitchen, chatting and cracking jokes as they worked on the turkey and trimmings. Louis watched how Fred made his Mum laugh, how effortlessly they seemed to fit together. It was strange but comforting to see her happy again.

Dinner was a success; the small dining table was packed with food and laughter. Even Hope appeared, weaving between their legs in search of scraps.

After the meal, they exchanged gifts. Louis gave his Mum a leather-bound notebook, which she immediately began flipping through, and a new chew toy for Lottie, who barked excitedly. Fred received a coffee table book on vintage cars, which he seemed genuinely thrilled about.

"This is perfect," Fred said, turning to Louis. "Thank you."

By early evening, it was time for them to leave. His Mum hugged him tightly. "You've done so well, Louis. This place is lovely. I'm proud of you."

Fred echoed her sentiment, shaking Louis's hand. "Happy Christmas. Hope we can do this again next year.

The warm hum of the fairy lights spilt from the living room into the small kitchen, where Louis stood rinsing plates at the sink. Fred had offered to help clean up, but Louis had waived him off, needing a few minutes to himself. The festive day had been a whirlwind of laughter and unexpected ease with Fred, yet now, in the quiet of the kitchen, the year's weight felt heavier.

He was stacking dishes on the drying rack when Mum walked in, her arms folded across her chest, her smile soft and reflective.

"Thought you might want some company," she said, leaning against the counter.

Louis chuckled lightly, setting the last plate down. "Did Fred send you in here to check on me?"

"No," she replied with a grin. "He's busy giving Lottie belly rubs on the couch. I came in because I wanted to talk to you."

The tone of her voice made Louis pause. He grabbed a tea towel, drying his hands as he turned to face her. "What's up?"

She hesitated, her fingers fidgeting with the edge of her cardigan. "I was just thinking about how far you've come since moving in here. I'm proud of you, Louis. This place—it's so you. You've done such a good job making it a home."

"Thanks, Mum," Louis said, his cheeks flushing. "It's been… nice having my own space."

She nodded but didn't drop her gaze. There was something else she wanted to say. After a beat, she took a step closer.

"You know," she began, her voice quieter now, "your 21st birthday is next month."

Louis laughed softly, a bit awkwardly. "Yeah, I've been trying not to think about it. Getting old and all that."

She swatted his arm gently. "Don't be daft. Twenty-one isn't old—it's a milestone. And I can't help but think about how happy you were when you turned eighteen. Do you remember that birthday?"

Louis's smile faded into something softer. He did. He could picture it so vividly: the Fred Perry jumper, the chocolate

179

cake with 18 candles, the excitement of heading to Glasgow with Carly.

"Yeah," he said after a long pause. "Feels like a lifetime ago, though."

His Mum leaned against the counter beside him, her gaze distant but warm. "You were so full of energy back then. Starting college, making plans to become a journalist... I've never seen you so excited about life. And that trip to London for the Doctor Who interview—you were buzzing for weeks."

Louis chuckled, but it was tinged with sadness. "I thought that was the start of everything. I really believed I was going to make it."

"You still can," she said softly.

He shook his head. "It's not that simple. Everything changed after that. COVID hit, college went online, and it felt like everything I'd been working for just... disappeared. I lost my momentum, Mum."

She reached out, placing a gentle hand on his shoulder. "I know it knocked you off balance, Louis. It was hard on everyone, but especially you. You were just finding your feet, and then the rug was pulled out from under you. But you're not stuck forever. You've got so much talent, so much heart. I still believe in you, even if you don't right now."

Louis swallowed hard, her words hitting him in places he'd tried to bury. "I don't even know where to start," he admitted, his voice barely above a whisper.

"Start where you are," she said simply. "You've got this flat. You've reconnected with your friends. Maybe it's time to think about what you want for yourself again."

He looked down at his hands, the tea towel clutched tightly in his grip. "What if I try, and I fail?"

"You might," she said honestly. "But you'll never know if you don't try. And even if you stumble, I'll be here, cheering you on. Always."

Her words brought a lump to his throat. He cleared it awkwardly, blinking away the sting of tears. "I just… I don't want to disappoint you."

"You've never disappointed me," she said, her voice firm. "Not once. What matters to me is that you're happy, Louis. And I think you'd be happiest chasing what you love—writing, telling stories, connecting with people. That's who you are."

Louis felt the tears welling up despite himself. He turned back to the sink, gripping the edge of the counter for a moment to steady himself.

"I was happy when I was doing all of that," he admitted, his voice thick with emotion. "I miss it."

"Then take it back," she said, stepping closer to him. "One step at a time. Start small—write something, anything. Just don't give up on yourself."

He nodded, his throat too tight to speak.

His Mum gave his shoulder a reassuring squeeze. "I want you to think about what you want for this next chapter. You've got so much ahead of you, Louis. Don't let fear hold you back."

Louis turned to face her, his eyes glistening. "Thanks, Mum. I don't know what I'd do without you."

"You'll never have to find out," she said with a soft smile, pulling him into a hug.

As they stood there in the small kitchen, the warmth of her embrace grounding him, Louis felt a flicker of hope—small but undeniable. Maybe he wasn't as lost as he thought. Maybe, just maybe, he could find his way back.

The sound of laughter from the living room drifted in, a soft reminder of the warmth surrounding him tonight. He pulled back from his Mum's hug, offering her a small, grateful smile.

"Go on," she said gently, nudging him toward the door. "Fred's probably let Lottie take over the couch by now."

Louis chuckled, wiping at his eyes. "Yeah, can't have that."

He followed her back to the living room, where Fred was laughing softly at something on TV, Lottie curled happily on his lap. Hope sat perched on the armrest, her green eyes observing the scene like a queen surveying her kingdom.

By early evening, his Mum and Fred had gathered their things to leave. As their footsteps faded down the hall, Louis lingered by the door, the flat now quiet save for the soft hum of the fairy lights and the occasional jingling of Lottie's collar fading into the distance.

Louis turned back to the living room, where Hope hopped onto his lap as he settled into the armchair by the tree. She purred contentedly, her warmth seeping into him as he stroked her fur. He let his gaze wander around the room—the twinkling lights on the tree, the faint scent of pine mingling with the lingering aroma of dinner, the paper snowflake he'd made as a boy hanging near the top.

He leaned his head back, staring up at the ceiling momentarily. Life wasn't perfect—it had been messy, unpredictable, and far from what he'd imagined. But tonight, in the glow of the decorations and the quiet hum of Hope's purring, he let himself believe that maybe the year ahead could be different.

For now, this moment of peace was enough.

The final hours of the year crept closer, and Louis's flat was buzzing with energy. The scent of mulled wine wafted from the kitchen, mingling with the faint spice of cinnamon candles. String lights looped around the walls and twinkled softly, casting a warm glow over the living room. It wasn't a grand party—Louis wasn't one for big crowds—but it was a celebration of reconnection, a gathering of people who mattered most to him.

Karen and Lauren had arrived first, bringing bottles of Prosecco and a platter of mini sausage rolls. Sarah wasn't far behind, her arms full of crisps, dips, and a bottle of whiskey she claimed was mandatory for Hogmanay. Carly followed, her laughter echoing through the hall as she nearly slipped on the icy pavement outside.

The last to arrive were Jamie, Ben, and Kirsty—a mix of old friends and outer-circle acquaintances Louis hadn't seen in ages. Jamie carried a Bluetooth speaker under one arm, promising a playlist that would "define the year," while Ben and Kirsty contributed a stack of party hats and noise makers.

Louis stood in the kitchen, arranging glasses on a tray, a nervous knot forming in his stomach. It had been a long time since he'd had so many people in his flat. Hope circled his feet, her tail flicking as she surveyed the chaos with mild interest.

"You all right in here?" Sarah's voice broke through his thoughts. She leaned against the doorframe, a glass of Prosecco already in hand.

Louis nodded, forcing a smile. "Yeah, just making sure everything's set."

"You're doing great," she said warmly, stepping closer. "It's nice, isn't it? Having everyone here."

"It is," he admitted, though the weight of hosting still lingered. "I just want it to go well."

Sarah squeezed his arm. "It already is."

"All right, Louis?"

Louis turned to see Ben slipping into the kitchen, a mischievous grin on his face and a bottle of beer dangling from his fingers.

"Yeah," Louis replied. "This has been a good night. Glad everyone came."

Ben leaned against the counter, glancing around the room before pulling something small from his pocket. He held it out on his palm—a small white pill.

"You want one?" Ben asked casually, his voice low.

Louis blinked, caught off guard. He wasn't naive—he knew Ben had dabbled in party drugs before. But this was the first time Ben had offered him anything directly.

"No, I don't do that shit anymore" Louis replied, his voice firm but steady.

"It's mellow—nothing heavy. You'll feel good, that's all." Ben replied with a shrug.

Louis stared at the pill, his thoughts swirling. The room behind them felt distant, the laughter and music muffled. He thought about how he'd been feeling recently stuck, unsure of his direction, and longing for something to shake him out of it.

But then his conversation with his Mum from Christmas echoed in his mind.

He shook his head, taking a step back. "Thanks, but I'm good."

Ben raised an eyebrow, clearly surprised. "You sure? It's New Year's Eve, mate. Live a little."

"I am," Louis said firmly. "But not like that, not this year"

For a moment, Ben looked like he might push further, but then he shrugged, tucking the pill back into his pocket. "Fair enough," he said, his tone light. "More for me."

As Ben turned and walked back into the living room, Louis let out a quiet breath, his grip tightening around his glass. He felt a flicker of pride—small, but real.

The night was a blur of laughter, music, and clinking glasses. Karen and Lauren had claimed the couch, deep in conversation about an upcoming holiday they were planning. Carly was busy quizzing Jamie about his job at the radio station, her eyes lighting up as he described the quirks of live broadcasting.

Kirsty had taken over the speaker, her playlist leaning heavily into 90s pop hits. Ben, ever the joker, was leading an impromptu dance competition in the centre of the room, his exaggerated moves earning cheers and groans in equal measure.

Louis drifted between groups, topping up drinks and laughing at Ben's antics. It felt good—natural, even—to have everyone together.

At one point, he found himself sitting on the arm of the couch beside Karen. She nudged him with her elbow, a knowing smile on her face.

"You're smiling," she said, taking a sip of her drink.

"Am I not allowed to smile?" he teased.

"No, but it's nice to see. You've been quieter these past few years. It's good to have this back—you back."

Her words struck a chord. Louis glanced around the room, the warmth of the scene settling over him like a blanket. "Thanks, Karen. That means a lot."

She grinned, raising her glass. "Here's to more of this in the new year."

As the clock edged closer to midnight, everyone gathered in the living room. Kirsty turned the music down, and Jamie queued up a classic Hogmanay favourite—Runrig's Loch Lomond.

Louis stood near the tree, a glass of whiskey in hand. Hope perched on the armrest beside him, watching the group with lazy curiosity.

Sarah tapped her glass with a spoon, quieting the room. "All right, since we're all here, I think it's only right to do a little reflection before we count down." She looked at Louis. "And since you're the host, you're up first!"

Louis groaned, laughing as the group cheered him on. He took a step forward, his pulse quickening. "All right, all right," he said, holding up his hands. "I'll keep it short."

He paused, his gaze sweeping across the faces in the room—friends he'd laughed with, drifted from, and now, slowly, reconnected with.

"This year hasn't been easy," he began, his voice steady but quiet. "The past few years haven't. For a while, I felt... stuck. Like I was watching everyone else move forward while I stayed in one place. But tonight, looking around this room, I feel lucky. Lucky to have people like you in my life."

The group clinked their glasses in agreement, a chorus of "Here, here!" filling the room.

Louis smiled, his throat tightening slightly. "So, here's to the new year—to moving forward, no matter how slow it feels. And to good friends, who make it all worth it."

The room erupted in cheers, and Karen pulled him into a hug. "That was perfect," she whispered.

The final seconds of the year ticked away, the group counting down together, voices rising with each number.

"Ten... nine... eight..."

Louis glanced around the room; his heart complete as the voices mingled in unison.

"Three... two... one... Happy New Year!"

The room exploded with cheers and laughter. Ben popped a party popper, sending confetti raining down over the group, while Kirsty blasted Auld Lang Syne from the speaker. Arms linked, they sang along, swaying in a circle that pulled Louis in without hesitation.

Hope meowed in protest from her perch, and Louis laughed, scooping her up as the song faded into another upbeat tune.

For the first time in years, he felt not just content, but hopeful. The future was uncertain, but it felt bright—full of possibilities he wasn't afraid to chase anymore.

As the night carried on, Louis sat by the tree, Hope curled in his lap and laughter ringing out around him.

CHAPTER TWELVE
BREAKING THE CHAINS

The January air was sharp but inside Louis's flat, warmth wrapped around him like a blanket. The morning sunlight filtered through the windows, casting long, soft shadows over the room, and it felt as if time had slowed, allowing Louis to savour the quiet moments before the rush of the day. His birthday had arrived—his 21st.

At noon, the doorbell rang, and Louis rushed to open it, greeted by the smiling faces of Gran and his Aunt Lorraine.

"Happy birthday, Louis!" his Gran said, stepping in first with a small, carefully wrapped gift in hand. Lorraine followed, a little more reserved, but her smile was just as wide as she took in the sight of his flat.

"Well, well, look at this place! I'm impressed," Aunt Lorraine said, glancing around the room. "It's cosy, Louis. Suits you."

Louis chuckled. "Yeah, it's a work in progress."

Lorraine had always been a constant figure in his childhood, though their paths had diverged over the years due to her busy work schedule. He'd always admired her strength and ambition, even if they hadn't kept in touch as much lately. It felt good to have her back in his life, if only for today.

"Don't let him fool you," Gran said, settling into the armchair with a grin. "He's been making it all look easy."

Aunt Lorraine pulled out a set of brightly coloured books from her bag, each one stacked carefully on top of the other. "I brought you these," she said, holding them out to him. "Heartstopper, the graphic novels. I heard there's a series on Netflix now—might be right up your alley."

Louis's eyes lit up. "I've heard of them! Thank you, Aunt Lorraine." He felt a surge of gratitude—simple gifts, but thoughtful and meaningful. His aunt had always known how to make him feel seen, even when they were distant.

"And from me," his Gran said, handing him a carefully wrapped picture frame. "I thought you could use this for your living room."

Louis took the frame, his smile deepening as he felt the weight of the gesture. It wasn't just the gifts that mattered—it was their presence, their support, their shared connection.

"Thanks, Gran," Louis said, leaning in to kiss her cheek. "It's perfect."

They spent the next few hours catching up, the conversation flowing easily as they reminisced about his childhood and talked about the future. Louis found himself talking more than he had in ages, revealing thoughts and plans he hadn't yet shared with anyone.

191

"This year, I'm going to focus on finding myself again," he said, looking between his Gran and aunt. "I've been stuck for too long, and it's time to do something about it."

Aunt Lorraine raised an eyebrow, clearly intrigued. "That's a good goal, Louis. Do you have anything in mind?"

Louis thought for a minute before answering, his eyes glinting with renewed purpose. "I don't know exactly, but I'm going to start by being more present, more active. I'm not sure where it'll lead, but I want to feel like I'm moving forward again."

His aunt nodded, her expression softening. "Well, I've got an idea, then. How about we climb Ben Lomond together in the summer? I've been wanting to get back into hiking, and I thought it might be fun to do it with you."

Louis's heart skipped a beat. He had always admired his aunt's adventurous spirit. "Yeah, I'd love that," he said, feeling a spark of excitement. It wasn't just about the hike—it was about the journey of reconnecting with family and the world outside his four walls.

Just as they were settling into a comfortable rhythm of conversation, the doorbell rang again. This time, it was his Mum, carrying a small gift bag and a warm smile.

"Happy birthday, darling," she said, wrapping him in a hug.

"Thanks, Mum," Louis said, his voice thick with emotion. He'd missed moments like this—simple, genuine moments of connection.

After a few more shared smiles and greetings, his Mum handed him an envelope, her eyes twinkling. "I've got something for you."

Louis looked at her curiously, tearing open the envelope. Inside was a card, but it was the small booking.com gift card with a note tucked underneath that caught his attention. He pulled it out slowly, unfolding the paper with care. The words that followed made his heart race:

'Go to London, Find that blue-eyed boy again. It's on me.'

For a minute, Louis stared at the note, the weight of the gesture settling in. He hadn't been to London since the interview with Nicholas Briggs, and the thought of returning—alone, to explore, to experience the city as he never had before—was thrilling. He could already imagine the streets, the landmarks, the quiet moments of reflection amidst the bustle.

Mum smiled gently, watching him. "I thought it might inspire you. Maybe you'll find your spark again, Louis. Sometimes a change of scenery is all it takes—a little solo adventure."

Louis swallowed hard; his throat tight with emotion. His mum's faith in him, her belief that he could find his way back to who he was, meant everything. "Mum… this is amazing. Thank you."

The room fell quiet, the weight of the conversation hanging in the air. It wasn't just about the trip—it was about the hope that it represented, the possibility of a new chapter. Louis realised as he looked around at the people who mattered most to him, that he was ready for it. Ready to start moving again.

The day stretched on, and they shared lunch, laughed, and reflected on the year ahead. Louis's heart felt full, the kind of fullness that only comes from a renewed sense of purpose, the love of family, and the belief that even though the future was uncertain, it was his to shape.

As evening descended, Louis's flat quieted down. Gran and Aunt Lorraine were the first to leave, hugging him tightly before stepping out into the January chill. His Mum lingered a little longer, chatting with Louis in the warmth of the living room before finally gathering her coat and bidding him goodnight with one last embrace.

"Have a wonderful night, Louis," she said, her eyes glinting with pride. "And don't forget to be safe"

"I will, Mum," Louis promised, watching her disappear down the hallway. The door closed softly, leaving him in the stillness of his flat. But the quiet didn't last long.

His phone buzzed. A message from Sarah popped up:

"Ready to relive the glory days? We're all here at First Ed, waiting on the birthday boy!"

A grin spread across Louis's face. It had been ages since he'd gone 'out, out' with the group—Sarah, Lauren, Karen, and Carly. Their meetups had been sporadic since life had taken them in different directions but tonight promised to be special.

He quickly changed into a sharp black button-up shirt and his favourite boots grabbed his coat and headed out into the crisp night air. The streets were alive with energy, and as he neared First Ed, he could already hear the familiar hum of laughter and music spilling out onto the pavement.

Pushing open the door, a chorus of cheers greeted him.

"There he is! The birthday boy!" Sarah waved him over, her vibrant personality commanding the room as usual. Lauren, Karen, and Carly joined in, wrapping him in hugs and shouting their well-wishes over the music.

"You're late!" Karen teased, sliding a pint across the table toward him. "We thought you'd gone and turned boring on us."

"Not a chance," Louis shot back, laughing as he took his seat. "

The night unfolded like a time capsule cracked open. They reminisced about school days, shared stories about their current lives, and laughed until their stomachs hurt. At one point, Lauren dared Louis to take the stage for karaoke. He hesitated for only a second before Sarah grabbed his arm.

"Oh, come on. You must do it. It's tradition!"

"Fine," Louis relented, shaking his head with a grin. "But only if you lot join me."

Seconds later, they were up on stage, the familiar opening synth of Depeche Mode's Enjoy the Silence vibrating through the bar. Louis took the lead, his voice steady and smooth, while the others chimed in for the chorus. The neon lights flickered softly across the karaoke stage, casting a faint glow over the group huddled around the small bar. He hadn't planned this. Hadn't planned to choose a song that would dig so deep, that would drag out the things he'd been ignoring for years. But there it was, in the heavy beat, in the melancholy melody—his Dad's absence was once again a shadow over the whole room, even though no one else seemed to notice it. The music swelled, and Louis inhaled deeply, letting the first few lyrics escape. His voice cracked slightly, the words feeling heavier than they had any right to.

"All I ever wanted, all I ever needed… is here, in my arms…"

His eyes scanned the room, landing on his friends, but they felt distant, too far away, like they couldn't understand what he was singing about. They didn't know what it felt like to have an empty chair at the table during your birthday, a seat that should have been filled by the person who taught you how to live with your flaws, who promised to be there for every milestone, every silly moment. Louis' throat tightened, but he pushed on. He couldn't stop now. The words were like a release, pulling him deeper into the feeling of loss that he had kept so carefully buried for so long. But now, as he stood there with his voice shaking, he realised just how much he'd been holding back.

As the song reached its peak, Louis closed his eyes, letting the final lines wrap around him. He didn't need to sing perfectly. He didn't need to pretend anymore. "Enjoy the silence," he whispered to himself, the words feeling more like a prayer than anything else.

The last note hung in the air, and for a moment, there was nothing but silence. But it wasn't empty. It wasn't cold. It was just… there. It was the space his Dad used to fill, and maybe, just maybe, it didn't need to be filled anymore. Louis took a deep breath and looked up, meeting the eyes of his friends. There was gentle applause, and a few cheers, but no one knew what he was feeling. And maybe they didn't need to. Maybe he didn't need them to. But for the first time, standing there alone, he felt like he had come to terms with it. His Dad wasn't there for him. But maybe, just maybe, it was okay to carry on without him.

Louis stepped down from the stage, flushed and grinning.

"You've still got it," Karen said, handing him a fresh drink.

"Barely," he replied, laughing. "But that was fun. I needed that."

"I'm just nipping to the toilet" Louis added, before leaving the table and walking towards the restrooms.

As Louis walked, soaking in the laughter and the light-hearted atmosphere of the bar, he noticed a familiar face across the room. Standing by the jukebox, talking with some of his friends, was Paul. Louis's stomach started doing flips. It had been a long time since he'd seen Paul, let alone thought about him. The last time their paths crossed hadn't ended well, and yet, here he was, standing in the same place as Louis and Sarah.

Their eyes locked, and Louis could feel the tension rise, the way his heart beat a little faster as memories flooded back. He tried to shake it off, but Paul was already making his way towards him, a grin on his face that seemed so out of place in the context of everything that had happened between them.

"Louis," Paul said, his voice smooth as ever. "It's been a while."

Louis nodded, forcing a smile, though a knot tightened in his chest. The others around him were still chatting, unaware of the encounter that was unfolding.

"I wasn't expecting to see you here," Louis replied, his tone neutral but firm, trying to avoid the warmth in his voice that Paul always seemed to pull out of him.

"Neither was I," Paul said with a slight chuckle, his eyes searching Louis's face. "But I'm glad I did."

Before Louis could respond, Paul leaned in, brushing his lips softly against Louis's cheek, then quickly moved to kiss him on the lips.

The world seemed to freeze. The familiar warmth of Paul's lips, the sense of closeness, all of it came rushing back to him. But in that split second, Louis felt a surge of clarity.

He pulled back, suddenly very aware of the distance between them—not just physically, but emotionally.

"You had your chance, Paul," Louis said, his voice steady but edged with emotion. "You broke my heart, and you broke my friend's heart. You made your choice, and now I must make mine."

Paul's expression faltered, and Louis could see the apology in his eyes. He could almost hear the words that Paul would try to say, but he didn't need to hear them. Not anymore.

"I'm sorry," Louis continued, taking a step back, feeling the weight of it all in his chest. "But you're not what I'm looking for this year. I'm looking for something different. For me."

The words hung in the air between them, and Paul didn't move. Louis didn't expect him to. He had said what needed to be said, and he felt a strange sense of relief run over him. The past was still there, lingering, but it no longer had the hold on him it once did.

"Enjoy your night, Paul," Louis added softly, before turning back to look at his friends, who were none the wiser before entering the toilets.

The night wore on with more laughter, stories, and a final toast to Louis as the clock inched closer to midnight.

"To finding ourselves again," Sarah said, raising her glass.

"To making it count," Louis added, clinking glasses with the group.

By the time he left the bar, the streets were quieter, the cold biting but not unwelcome. Louis walked home slowly, replaying the evening in his mind. His heart felt light, buoyed by the joy of reconnecting and the promise of new beginnings.

When he finally reached his flat, he stepped inside, the silence greeting him like an old friend. He slipped out of his boots and sank onto the sofa, the memories of the day washing over him. From the warmth of family to the laughter of old friends, it had been everything he needed—a reminder of the love and support surrounding him, and the strength within him to face whatever lay ahead.

For the first time in a long while, Louis felt a spark of excitement for the future. He closed his eyes, a small smile on his lips as sleep began to take over, the strains of Enjoy the Silence still echoing in his mind.

The following morning, Louis sat on his sofa, the glow of his phone screen illuminating his face. He felt a rush of excitement as he scrolled through flight options, each one a step closer to the adventure he was planning. He could almost picture himself walking through the busy streets of London, taking in the sights, feeling a sense of freedom that had been missing for far too long.

He clicked a flight leaving in August, the dates perfect for what he had in mind. Louis was not sure what he was hoping for, but there was something about London that felt like a fresh start, a place to reconnect with the world outside the walls of his flat.

He typed in his details, confirming the flight time, and then, with a deep breath, moved to the next part: booking his accommodation.

Westminster—he'd always been fascinated by that area of London. The history, the energy, the iconic landmarks. It was the perfect place to be based for his trip. He found a hostel, simple but with great reviews. It wasn't luxurious, but it was affordable and centrally located. Three nights would be just enough to take in the city at his own pace. The thought of waking up each day in the heart of London, surrounded by so much life, felt invigorating.

His Mum had put the money on the booking.com gift card for it, Louis hesitated for a second, his finger hovering over the payment button before he clicked it.

The confirmation screen appeared:

Your booking is confirmed! You're all set for your stay in Westminster.

A wave of relief washed over him. It was happening. The next few months would fly by, and before he knew it, he'd be standing on the streets of London, ready to take on whatever came his way.

He smiled to himself, knowing his Mum would be thrilled when she heard. She'd been supportive, even when things hadn't been going well. This trip, this adventure, felt like a step forward, a way to reclaim a part of himself that had been lost. And he knew, no matter what happened, he was doing this for him.

Louis sat his phone down, lying back on his sofa. For the first time in a while, he felt a genuine spark of excitement for the future.

London was just the beginning.

CHAPTER THIRTEEN
MUNROS AND MINI BREAKS

The summer morning air was sharp and invigorating as Louis stepped into Aunt Lorraine's car, a flask of coffee warming his hands. It was just past seven, and the sky was beginning to lighten with the first hints of dawn. Lorraine greeted him with a bright smile, her energy contagious.

"Ready for this, kiddo?" she asked, adjusting her sunglasses even though the sun hadn't fully risen.

"As ready as I'll ever be," Louis replied, his grin matching hers.

The drive to Ben Lomond was serene, winding through Scotland's stunning countryside. Mist curled over the Lochs, and the hills were cloaked in shadowy greens and greys. Louis sipped his coffee, feeling the nervous excitement building in his chest. Hiking wasn't something he did often, but the idea of challenging himself—of experiencing something new—was exhilarating.

As they approached the base of Ben Lomond, the sun broke through the clouds, casting a golden glow over the landscape. Lorraine parked the car, and they stepped out into the cool, fresh air.

"Let's take it slow," Lorraine said, strapping on her backpack. She handed Louis a water bottle and an energy bar. "It's not a race—it's about enjoying the journey."

Louis nodded, slinging his backpack over his shoulder. They started up the trail at a steady pace, the gravel crunching underfoot.

The climb was challenging but manageable, with the trail winding through heather-covered slopes and patches of rocky outcrops. As they ascended, the sun climbed higher, its warmth chasing away the morning chill. Lorraine pointed out landmarks, her knowledge of the area clear.

"That's Loch Lomond," she said, gesturing to the shimmering expanse of water below. "Beautiful, isn't it? This view always reminds me why I love Scotland."

Louis paused to take it in, his breath catching at the sheer beauty of it. "It's stunning," he murmured.

As the hours passed, their conversation ebbed and flowed naturally. They talked about Lorraine's hiking adventures, and Louis's plans for London, and even swapped childhood memories. The bond that had frayed over the years began to feel stronger with each step.

As they reached the summit, the sun was high in the sky, and the heat of the day was noticeable. Louis stood at the peak, gazing out at the panoramic view. Rolling hills stretched into the distance, dotted with tiny lochs glinting like scattered jewels. The world felt vast and infinite.

"This is incredible," he said, his voice hushed with awe.

Lorraine sat on a nearby rock, pulling out a flask of tea. "Worth the climb, isn't it?" she said, handing him a cup.

Louis nodded, sipping the tea and letting the views sink in. The wind ruffled his hair, and he felt truly alive for the first time in a long while—like he was part of something bigger than himself.

The trek down was easier, though their legs protested with each step. When they reached the car, they were both ravenous. Lorraine pulled out a cooler from the boot, revealing sandwiches wrapped in foil.

"Not fancy," she said, handing him one. "But there's nothing better than a simple lunch after a hike."

Louis bit into his sandwich, savouring the taste. The simplicity of the meal, paired with the satisfaction of the climb, made it feel like a feast.

They sat on the grassy slope by the car, the warmth of the sun on their backs.

"So," Lorraine began, glancing at Louis, "how are you feeling about London tomorrow?"

Louis took a moment before answering, his gaze fixed on the horizon. "Excited, I think. Nervous too. It's been a while since I've done something just for me."

Lorraine nodded, her expression thoughtful. "That's the whole point, isn't it? To step out of your comfort zone and see where it takes you. I think it's exactly what you need."

"Yeah," Louis said, smiling. "I think so too."

They packed up and began the drive home, the conversation turning to lighter topics as the miles slipped by.

By the time Lorraine dropped Louis off at his flat, the day's exhaustion had set in but so had a deep sense of contentment.

Inside his flat, Louis kicked off his boots and sank into the sofa. His muscles ached in a satisfying way, and his mind was calm. He thought about the day—the climb, the views, the connection with Lorraine—and felt a swell of gratitude.

The hike had been more than just a physical challenge; it was a reminder of his resilience, of the beauty in taking things step by step. And as he looked ahead to his solo trip to London, he felt something he hadn't felt in a long time: hope.

The city awaited him, a canvas for his next chapter. But for now, he let himself rest, his heart full and his mind at peace.

The soft buzz of Louis's phone woke him at precisely 4 a.m., though he had barely slept in anticipation. He rolled over in bed, his eyes landing on the corner of his room where his rucksack sat ready, along with a neatly folded outfit and his passport perched on top. Today was the day.

Excitement surged through him, erasing any grogginess. He jumped out of bed and headed straight for the shower, letting the warm water jolt him fully awake. Emerging refreshed, he pulled on his outfit—a crisp white T-shirt, blue jean shorts, and his pristine white-and-blue Nike Air Force Ones. It was simple but unmistakably him.

As he moved through the flat, the quiet morning was broken only by the soft meows of Hope, his sleek ginger cat, weaving around his legs.

"All right, Hope," he said, crouching to scratch behind her ears. "Don't miss me too much, okay?"

He filled her bowl with fresh food and water, then double-checked the weeks' worth of supplies he'd set out for her cat sitter. Satisfied, he slung his rucksack over one shoulder, gave Hope a final affectionate rub, and stepped out into the hallway.

Louis climbed the stairs to the top floor, where his neighbour Tracy lived. She'd kindly agreed to watch Hope for him while he was away. He slipped his spare house key through her letterbox.

"Thanks, Tracy," he muttered under his breath, already imagining Hope curled up on her lap.

Descending back to his flat, Louis pulled out his phone and fired off a quick text to Liz – a newfound friend he had become close with throughout the past year.

Ready to go! See you soon.

Within minutes, Liz's car pulled up outside his building. He locked the door behind him, crouched one last time to say goodbye to Hope through the window, and headed out to meet her.

"Good morning, London-bound traveller!" Liz called as Louis climbed into the passenger seat, her eyes sparkling with excitement.

"Morning," Louis said, grinning as he tossed his rucksack into the backseat.

Liz could not contain her enthusiasm. "I'm so proud of you! Your big London adventure, how does it feel?"

"A little surreal, to be honest," Louis admitted. "I'm excited, but I've got butterflies, too."

Liz laughed a warm and encouraging sound. "You'll be fine. You've got this!"

As they drove through the quiet pre-dawn streets, Louis pulled out his phone to show her a playlist he had curated for the trip.

"Look at this," he said, scrolling through the songs. "Some Taylor Swift, a bit of Elton John—it's got everything."

Liz glanced over and snorted. "That is so Louis-coded. If I didn't know better, I'd say you made this just to impress yourself."

"Of course I did," Louis said, laughing.

The drive passed quickly, and before long, they were pulling up to Glasgow Airport. Liz parked and insisted on walking him inside.

"You're going to do great," Liz said as they reached the check-in area. "Just remember to breathe. And text me when you land!"

Louis nodded, his nerves bubbling to the surface as the reality of flying alone hit him. He hugged Liz tightly. "Thanks for everything. You're the best."

"I know," she replied with a wink. "Now go on—your adventure awaits!"

Inside, Louis found his way around the airport with ease. He joined the queue for security. As he moved, his thoughts briefly wandered as to why this trip mattered so much. It was not just about travelling; it was a step toward independence, proof to himself that he could navigate the world on his own terms. After a year of ups and downs, this felt like reclaiming a part of himself he'd almost lost.

Security was uneventful, though Louis found himself triple-checking every pocket and zipper to make sure he hadn't forgotten anything important – or absentmindedly smuggled through some sort of gun. Once through, he wandered into the duty-free area, marvelling at the rows of luxury goods he couldn't afford. The scent of expensive perfume mingled with freshly brewed coffee from the nearby cafés, creating an oddly comforting atmosphere.

Eventually, he found a quiet corner near the boarding gates and grabbed a sandwich for breakfast. As he ate, he popped in his earbuds and queued up his playlist. The familiar melodies of Taylor Swift calmed his nerves as he watched the gate's activity. His phone buzzed with a notification at precisely 6:45 a.m.:

Flight now boarding.

Louis stood, slung his rucksack over his shoulder, and made his way to the gate. He scanned his ticket, marvelling at how easy the process was, and walked out onto the runway.

The early summer sun, bathed the scene in a warm glow, casting long shadows across the tarmac. Louis climbed the stairs to the plane, his heart racing—not with fear, but with exhilaration.

Inside, he found his seat by the window and settled in, tucking his bag beneath the seat in front of him. Around him, the plane filled quickly, mostly with business travellers chatting quietly or flipping through emails on their phones.

As the plane taxied down the runway and lifted into the air, Louis pressed his forehead against the window, watching the world shrink below him. The rolling hills and scattered lochs of Scotland stretched out like a patchwork quilt, the morning light painting everything in soft hues of gold and green.

The hum of the engines was oddly soothing, and before long, Louis drifted off into a light nap.

The captain's voice crackled over the intercom, announcing their approach to Stansted Airport. Louis stirred, rubbing his eyes as the plane began its descent. He looked out the window, the patchwork of London's outskirts coming into view.

Once on the ground, Louis made his way through the bustling terminal, following the signs to the National Express bus stop. With his ticket scanned and his rucksack stowed in the luggage compartment, he boarded the bus and took a window seat near the middle. The next leg of his journey was set to be just over an hour, and Louis was eager to take it all in.

CHAPTER FOURTEEN
FLICKERS OF A NEW HORIZON

As the bus left Stansted behind, the scenery transitioned from the rolling fields of the English countryside to the industrial outskirts of London. The sun climbed higher, illuminating the landscape. Louis watched the change with fascination, reflecting on his last trip to London in 2020. The memory of masked faces and quiet streets felt distant now. This time, the world felt open and alive again.

He checked his phone, pulling up the details of his booking. His hostel was in Pimlico, Westminster—a budget-friendly choice that made him nervous. Louis had never stayed in a hostel before and wasn't entirely sure what to expect. Sharing a room with strangers felt intimidating, but it was all part of the adventure.

The bus entered the heart of the city, and Louis couldn't help but draw parallels between the vibrant streets and his first visit. The energy was electric, the buildings towering and full of character. When the bus pulled into London Liverpool Street, Louis stepped off and looked around, immediately spotting a restaurant with a sign that read 'Dirty Dicks'

He burst out laughing, the name striking him as absurdly funny. His amusement didn't last long, though, as his eyes caught sight of the Gherkin building towering in the distance. Its unique, modern design left him in awe. He stood there for a moment, soaking in the juxtaposition of historic and contemporary architecture, feeling small but exhilarated.

With a renewed sense of excitement, Louis grabbed his rucksack and began making his way toward the Underground, ready to navigate the final stretch to Pimlico. The adventure had truly begun.

Louis took the Underground with ease, changing lines twice and finally arriving at Pimlico Station. From there, it was a short walk to his hostel on Belgrave Road. The tree-lined street was quieter than he expected, offering a small reprieve from the city's hustle and bustle.

When he arrived at the hostel, he checked in and climbed the stairs to his room. Inside, he found six red bunk beds artfully arranged. To his relief, he was the first to arrive and quickly claimed a bottom bunk. After freshening up, he stored his luggage in the locked cage beneath his bed, feeling a mix of nervousness and excitement. Staying in a hostel was a new experience, but he was ready for whatever the trip had in store.

Louis flopped back onto the bottom bunk, his body sinking into the firm mattress. Despite the morning's excitement, a wave of boredom washed over him. The unfamiliarity of the hostel was both exhilarating and strange. He stared at the underside of the bunk above him, the peeling paint on the metal frame doing little to entertain him.

With a deep breath, he stood up and grabbed his jacket. With no destination in mind, he decided a walk would clear his head.

As he stepped outside, the warm London air hit him. He wandered through the streets, his footsteps echoing softly in the otherwise quiet afternoon. The city was still alive, but it felt far removed as if he were walking in his own little bubble, detached from the rush of the world around him.

The walk took him through the heart of Westminster, past the historic buildings and the grand monuments that seemed to tower over him, their stone faces glowing faintly in the streetlight. It was peaceful here, like this part of the city was asleep, and the only company was the sound of his shoes against the pavement.

Eventually, he found himself outside The Feathers, a quaint pub tucked away on a side street. Without thinking too much about it, he stepped inside.

Inside, the pub was cosy, the air thick with the smell of wood smoke and ale. The chatter of patrons filled the space, and Louis found a quiet corner where he could nurse a drink. As he settled into his seat, his eyes wandered around the room. That's when he saw Steven—a man in his early thirties, with a scruffy beard and an easy smile. Steven's eyes caught Louis's, and a silent acknowledgement passed between them.

"Is this seat taken?" Steven asked, his voice warm.

Louis shook his head, offering a small smile of his own. "No, go ahead."

Steven slid into the seat across from him, his presence somehow comforting and intriguing. They exchanged a few casual words, the kind of small talk that came quickly in a place like this, but as the minutes passed, their conversation began to feel more genuine. Louis found himself relaxing, the tension in his shoulders easing.

"So, Scotland," Steven began, setting the glass down with a soft clink. "I've been up to Glasgow a few times for work. I quite like it. Great food, interesting people, and there's something about the vibe—it feels real, you know?"

Louis couldn't help but chuckle, swirling his gin and lemonade. "Really? Glasgow? It's all right, I guess, but compared to London, it's so… boring. Everything shuts down early, and the nightlife is decent at best. Here, it's like the city never sleeps."

Steven raised an eyebrow, intrigued by Louis's bluntness. "Boring? That's a strong word. Sounds like you've got ambitious standards. What's so bad about it?"

Louis leaned back in his chair, grinning. "Don't get me wrong—it's fine. But I've lived near Glasgow my whole life. It's predictable. London feels alive like something exciting is always just around the corner. Plus, have you seen the architecture here? The Gherkin alone is more interesting than half of Glasgow's city centre."

215

Steven laughed, shaking his head. "All right, you've got me there. London is a beast of its own. But you might be selling Glasgow short. Maybe you just need to see it through a different lens—like mine." He gave Louis a playful wink, causing Louis to blush slightly.

They talked for another hour, their conversation flowing easily as the drinks kept coming. Louis found himself loosening up, laughing more freely with Steven, who had a knack for storytelling. He recounted tales of working in Westminster, peppered with dry humour and the occasional mischievous grin.

Louis couldn't help but be drawn to the man's confidence—it was magnetic. By their third round of drinks, Steven had nestled closer, his knee brushing against Louis's under the table.

Steven patted him lightly on the back, the faintest hint of mischief in his smile. "What do you say I show you around? I know a bar in Chinatown that's not far from here, pass a few landmarks on the way."

Louis nodded, his heart still racing. "Lead the way."

Steven led the way out of the pub, and Louis followed eagerly. They stepped into the cool evening air, the city alive with lights and sounds. Steven turned toward a nearby tunnel that disappeared beneath the street.

"This way," he said over his shoulder, flashing Louis a smile.

The tunnel echoed with their footsteps as they walked side by side, their conversation light but filled with unspoken energy. Emerging on the other side, they found themselves near Hyde Park, the vast expanse of greenery bathed in the soft glow of streetlights.

Steven gestured toward the park's iconic lake, where swans glided effortlessly across the water. "You ever been here before?"

Louis shook his head, his gaze fixed on the serene scene. "No. It's beautiful, though."

Steven chuckled. "Wait until you see what's next."

They strolled along the edge of the park, crossing quiet streets until the imposing façade of Buckingham Palace came into view. The golden gates gleamed under the city lights, and Louis paused to take it all in.

"Does it ever feel surreal living here?" Louis asked, glancing at Steven.

"Sometimes," Steven admitted, leaning casually against the railing. "But the magic comes back when you're showing someone else around. Like now."

From there, they wandered down toward the back of Downing Street, the seat of power tucked discreetly behind guarded gates. Louis marvelled at the thought of being so close to where world-changing decisions were made.

"Not quite as grand as the palace," Steven quipped, "but it's got its charm."

Louis laughed. "I guess it's more... practical."

They continued their journey, the busy energy of the city growing as they approached Piccadilly Circus. Neon signs illuminated the square, casting vibrant colours over the throngs of people weaving through the streets.

"Now this," Steven said, spreading his arms, "is London."

Louis pulled out his phone. "We have to take a picture here."

Steven grinned, and they posed in front of the famous screens, the chaos of the city captured in the background. Louis couldn't help but feel a pang of pride as he snapped the photo—a moment that felt like it belonged to a different, more adventurous version of himself.

Their journey ended in the heart of Chinatown, where lanterns strung across the narrow streets glowed warmly, their soft light reflecting off red and gold shop signs. The air was rich with the scent of dumplings, roasted meats, and sweet pastries.

"This place is amazing," Louis said, spinning in place to take it all in.

Steven led him into a cosy bar tucked away on a side street. The walls were adorned with vintage Chinese posters, and soft jazz music played in the background.

Over their final drink—a whiskey sour for Steven and another pink gin and lemonade for Louis—they reminisced about their impromptu adventure.

"You know," Steven said, swirling his glass, "you've got a spark about you, Louis. Don't lose it."

Louis smiled, feeling a warmth that went beyond the alcohol. "Thanks. Tonight's been... incredible."

As they finished their drinks, the reality of parting ways began to settle in. They stepped outside, the streets quieter now but still alive with possibility.

"Well," Steven said, adjusting his jacket. "This is where I leave you."

Louis nodded; his heart heavy but full at the same time. "Thanks for everything. I won't forget it."

Steven smiled, reaching out to shake Louis's hand before pulling him into a quick, unexpected hug. "Take care of yourself, kid."

And with that, Steven disappeared into the crowd, leaving Louis standing beneath the lanterns of Chinatown, the city stretching out before him, vibrant and full of promise.

By 9 p.m., Louis was back in the hostel, his stomach full but his thoughts restless. Dinner had been a simple affair—a mac and cheese ready meal from Sainsbury's. He'd microwaved it in the communal kitchen, where the faint smell of spices and reheated pasta hung in the air. While waiting for the ping of the microwave, his eyes caught the events board on the wall.

Movie and Games Night: Lounge, 9 PM

The listing piqued his interest. He needed something to do, a way to fill the rest of the evening.

With his mac and cheese devoured, Louis grabbed a bottle of water and made his way to the lounge. The room was cosy, dotted with bean bags, mismatched chairs, and a projector casting the opening credits of Bridget Jones's Diary onto a pull-down screen.

Louis smiled to himself as he took a seat on one of the sofas. Bridget Jones's Diary was one of his and his Mum's favourite films. They'd watched it countless times together, quoting lines and laughing at Bridget's endless misadventures.

As the movie played, more people trickled in. A group of backpackers near the back laughed loudly at the scene where Bridget slid down the fireman's pole, her knickers flashing for all to see.

"Classic," someone said beside him.

Louis turned to see a girl with sun-kissed skin, freckles, and a mane of blonde hair tied into a messy bun. She looked to be in her early twenties, her Australian accent unmistakable.

"Classic disaster," Louis replied, grinning.

She laughed, the sound warm and inviting. "I'm Stella," she said, holding out her hand.

"Louis," he replied, shaking it.

They started chatting, their conversation flowing as naturally as if they'd known each other for years. Stella was travelling solo, having just come from a week in Edinburgh, and was now ticking London off her list before heading to mainland Europe.

"It's nice to meet someone else travelling alone," she said, her blue eyes sparkling. "Sometimes hostels can be a bit... cliquey."

Louis nodded. "Yeah, but it's been nice so far. And London's... something else."

Stella tilted her head. "You know what would blow your mind? The Thames at night. There's a boat that goes down to Canary Wharf. It leaves late, and the city's incredible all lit up."

"Canary Wharf?" Louis's ears perked up. "That was in Doctor Who. The Cybermen were there!"

Stella chuckled. "I'll take your word for it. But trust me, it's worth seeing. Fancy it?"

Louis hesitated just for a second. He hadn't planned on going out again tonight, but the idea of seeing London from the river, especially with someone like Stella, was too good to pass up.

"Yeah, why not?" he said, excitement igniting within him.

They left the lounge before the movie ended, stopping by their rooms to grab jackets. Stella led the way, pulling up directions on her phone as they navigated the streets toward the dock. The city felt alive in a unique way at night—quieter but still humming with energy.

When they reached the boat, the Thames stretched out before them, dark and rippling, reflecting the city lights in a dazzling display. They boarded just as the last passengers were settling in.

The boat glided down the river, passing iconic landmarks bathed in golden light. Big Ben, the London Eye, Tower Bridge— all of it seemed surreal to Louis like he was in a dream. Stella pointed out landmarks, sharing the knowledge she'd picked up from her travels.

When Canary Wharf came into view, Louis's breath caught. The towering glass skyscrapers shimmered like beacons in the night, their reflections stretching endlessly across the water.

"This is amazing," Louis exclaimed, leaning on the railing.

"Told you," Stella replied, her grin wide.

They snapped photos and shared stories as the boat gently rocked beneath them. For Louis, this wasn't just sightseeing—it was an adventure, a memory he'd carry long after he left London.

When the boat docked, they made their way back to the hostel, their conversation filled with laughter and plans for the next day. As they parted ways for the night, Louis felt a warmth in his chest—a mix of gratitude and hope.

London was turning out to be more than just a destination; it was a place where anything felt possible.

After their magical nighttime boat ride down the Thames, Louis and Stella strolled to the Canary Wharf Underground Station. The sleek, modern design of the station reminded Louis of something out of a science fiction film, its wide-open spaces and metallic finishes echoing the futuristic feel of the area.

They boarded the Jubilee Line, and the train hummed softly as it sped through the tunnels beneath London. Stella leaned her head back, clearly worn out but happy, while Louis stared out at the occasional blur of station lights as they zipped past.

"So, tomorrow?" Stella asked sleepily, glancing at him.

"Let's see where the day takes us." Louis replied with a grin.

When the train reached Green Park, they switched to the Victoria Line, which carried them toward Pimlico. The crowds thinned as the journey went on, and by the time they reached their stop, only a handful of passengers remained.

"Night, Louis," she said as they exited the station and headed back to the hostel.

"Night, Stella," he replied, his words laced with gratitude.

In his dorm, Louis made his way to his bunk, careful not to disturb his sleeping roommates. He pulled off his trainers,

223

plugged in his phone, and sank into the surprisingly comfortable mattress.

As he pulled the blanket up, he let the day's events wash over him—Steven at the pub, the majestic sights of London lit up at night, and his newfound friendship with Stella. It was a whirlwind but in the best way possible.

The gentle hum of the city outside lulled him to sleep, and for the first time in a while, Louis felt truly content.

Louis woke up with a start, the sticky warmth of the London night still clinging to him. His skin felt clammy, and the faint hum of the small fan in the corner of the room did little to alleviate the lingering heat. He groaned, sitting up and glancing at his phone. 9:00 AM. He'd slept well, though the sweat suggested it had been too warm to be entirely comfortable. London was certainly different from back home—the heat, the buzz, and even the energy felt heightened. Yesterday, it had been 22 degrees and today promised to be just as warm.

Sliding out of the bunk, Louis grabbed his shower things and shuffled toward the shared bathroom. The cubicle was small and cramped, but the blast of cool water was a relief. He stood under it for a few extra moments, letting it wake him up properly. Once done, he towelled off quickly, tied his hair into place, and headed back to his room.

For the day ahead, Louis picked out a pair of black jeans, a white t-shirt, and one of his favourites: a white over shirt adorned with delicate floral patterns on each side. It was a light, breezy outfit, ideal for walking around the city without looking like a tourist. He gave himself a quick glance in the mirror, smiling slightly at the reflection. He felt good—refreshed and ready.

Sliding on his trainers and checking that his phone and wallet were safely in his pockets, Louis grabbed a reusable water bottle and then left the hostel. The warmth of the morning sun hit him at once, and he took a deep breath of the fresh city air. His plan today? A visit to Oxford Circus for some light shopping, and a little exploring.

The streets along Belgrave Road were bustling as usual. Buses passed by in flashes of red, tourists ambled about with maps, and locals zipped by on bikes. Louis loved the mix of energy in London. It felt alive in a way he wasn't used to, and he couldn't help but smile as he headed toward Pimlico Station.

The Tube ride was quick and efficient, and before he knew it, he was climbing the steps to Oxford Circus. As he emerged, the city seemed to grow louder and more chaotic. The streets were packed with tourists snapping photos, office workers in sharp suits rushing to meetings, and shoppers darting between stores with bags in hand.

The energy was electric, and Louis soaked it all in as he navigated the crowds. He finally made his way to Selfridges; the grand department store he had only ever heard about online. Walking inside felt like stepping into another world.

The ground floor was a maze of jewellery counters, perfume displays, and luxury makeup brands, all lit with soft, golden lighting. Louis moved through it all in awe, glancing at the high-end products as he made his way upstairs. The tech gadgets, sleek designer clothing, and the sprawling John Lewis section caught his attention, but he kept going. He had a destination in mind: the Jellycat store on the top floor.

He'd seen Jellycats everywhere on TikTok, their plush designs becoming something of an obsession for people his age. Now, standing in front of the display, Louis felt a childlike giddiness. The shelves were lined with soft animals in all shapes and sizes. After careful consideration, his eyes landed on Fergus the Frog. Fergus had an irresistibly squishy design, with big, friendly eyes and a smile that seemed to radiate cheerfulness.

Without hesitation, Louis made his purchase, and as he left the store with Fergus tucked safely in a bright yellow bag, he felt like he'd gained a new little companion for his London adventure.

After Selfridges, his stomach began to rumble, so he ducked into a nearby pizza spot. The smell of fresh dough and melted cheese was too good to resist. Ordering a pepperoni pizza, Louis found a small table by the window and savoured every bite. The combination of rich cheese, tangy tomato sauce, and the slight kick of pepperoni was perfect. It reminded him of the pizzas he'd share with his family on Saturday nights as a kid.

Feeling content and full, he decided to wander into an HMV store he'd noticed across the street. The rows of vinyl records, band posters, and quirky memorabilia drew him in, and he found himself lost in nostalgia. He picked up a small badge and a postcard—cheap, meaningful keepsakes to remember the trip. At one point, he spotted a Cards Against Humanity game, which brought a smile to his face. It reminded him of late-night games at sleepovers, where laughter would fill the room. He debated buying it but decided to leave it for now.

By midday, the weight of his purchases—and the growing heat—was starting to catch up to him. The busy streets seemed even more packed, and Louis felt the fatigue of navigating through crowds. Deciding it was time to take a break, he headed back to the Tube station and made his way to Pimlico.

The walk back along Belgrave Road was slower this time, the warmth of the afternoon sun urging him to move at a leisurely pace. When he reached the hostel, the coolness of his room was a welcome relief. Carefully unpacking his purchases, he placed Fergus the Frog on his pillow, where the plush toy sat like a cheerful guardian of his bed.

Louis stretched out, letting the quiet of his room envelop him as he thought back over the morning. London had been everything he'd hoped for and more—a place of endless possibilities and surprises. With a contented sigh, he closed his eyes, ready to recharge for whatever the rest of the day might hold.

Later. Louis stepped into the hall, still smiling to himself about Fergus the Frog when a familiar voice caught his attention. "Louis, hey!"

He turned to see Stella, her hair was pulled into a messy ponytail, and she looked effortlessly cool, dressed in a denim jacket and a band tee.

"Fancy seeing you here!" she said, pulling him into a quick hug.

"Stella!" Louis grinned, genuinely glad to see her.

"Are you busy? What do you say we grab some booze from the shop down the road and have a drink? There's a group in the kitchen—they seem chill."

Louis hesitated for only a second before nodding. "Sounds good to me."

They headed to the local shop, falling back into the easy rhythm of conversation. Stella grabbed a bottle of vodka and a pack of mixers while Louis picked up a six-pack of cider.

Back at the hostel kitchen, the energy was lively. A mismatched group of travellers was seated around the large communal table, laughing and chatting over drinks. Stella waved them over.

"Hey, mind if we join?" she asked, setting the bottles down.

"Of course!" said a blonde girl with a wide smile and a thick German accent. "I'm Ena. This is Chris, and that's Tyler."

Louis's eyes fell on Tyler, who was leaning back in his chair, a beer in hand. His blonde hair caught the fluorescent light, and his smile—bright and confident—made Louis's stomach do a small flip.

Tyler raised his drink in greeting. "Nice to meet you, man." His voice carried a slight drawl that only added to his charm.

"Nice to meet you, too," Louis managed, feeling uncharacteristically flustered.

The drinks flowed freely as introductions turned into stories. Chris, from Washington State, shared tales of hiking in the Cascades, while Ena described her travels through Europe. Tyler chipped in with stories from Florida—days spent on the beach and nights partying in Miami.

Louis found himself drawn to Tyler, not just by his looks but by the way he carried himself, his laugh, and the easy way he made everyone feel included.

At one point, Louis mentioned the Cards Against Humanity game he'd seen earlier. "I almost bought it this morning. Would've been perfect for tonight."

Stella checked her phone. "It's not that late. The shop might still be open."

Louis hesitated. "I could run back and grab it."

"I'll come with you," Tyler offered, setting his drink down.

Louis blinked, his heart skipping a beat. "You sure?"

"Yeah, why not? Could use some air," Tyler said, flashing that dazzling smile.

The two of them left the hostel, stepping into the warm night. The streets were alive with performers, tourists, and the hum of the city. As they walked toward the station, Louis found it easy to talk to Tyler.

"So, what brings you to London?" Louis asked.

"Honestly? A bit of everything. I've always wanted to see Europe, and I figured, why not start with the UK?" Tyler shrugged; his hands tucked into his pockets. "What about you?"

"Needed a break from everything back home," Louis admitted.

Tyler nodded, his expression softening. "Yeah, I get that."

The train ride was quick, and soon they were back at Oxford Circus, weaving through the bustling streets. Street performers played music, and the city felt alive in an unusual way at night.

"It's crazy here. So much energy." Tyler said as they found the shop.

Louis laughed. "It's why I love it."

They found the game easily, and Tyler grabbed it from the shelf. "Got it. Let's head back and show them how it's done."

The return to the hostel was just as lively, the streets glowing under streetlights. Back in the kitchen, the group cheered at the sight of the game.

"Let the chaos begin," Stella declared, pouring more drinks.

The game started tame - but quickly devolved into raucous laughter as the alcohol kicked in. Louis couldn't help but steal glances at Tyler, who was effortlessly funny and quick-witted, his laugh infectious.

The night wore on, and the group of strangers grew louder, and Louis felt a warmth he hadn't felt in a while. Surrounded by new friends and sitting next to Tyler, he let himself enjoy the moment, letting go of the weight he'd been carrying for so long.

As the laughter began to wind down and the energy in the kitchen softened, Tyler turned to Louis with an easy smile. "So, what are your plans tomorrow?"

Louis shrugged. "No real plans yet. Figured I'd just explore some more."

Tyler tilted his head slightly. "Well, if you're up for it, I was thinking of checking out Big Ben and Tower Bridge. Could be fun to go together."

Louis felt a flicker of excitement at the idea. "Yeah, I'd like that."

"Cool," Tyler said, pulling out his phone. "Here, let's swap Instas so we can figure it out in the morning."

Louis fumbled for his phone, quickly finding Tyler's account and following him back. Tyler's feed was a mix of travel snaps, beach photos, and silly selfies with friends, each one making him seem even more charismatic.

"All right, I'll message you in the morning," Tyler said, slipping his phone into his pocket.

"Sounds good." Louis smiled, feeling a strange mix of nerves and excitement.

By then, the rest of the group was starting to pack up, their voices quieter now as the night caught up with them. Ena yawned dramatically. "Okay, I am done for the night. See you all tomorrow, maybe."

Chris chuckled. "Yeah, I think I've hit my limit, too. Night, everyone."

The group said their goodbyes, leaving Louis and Tyler lingering. Tyler stood up and stretched, his shirt riding up slightly, revealing a hint of his toned stomach. Louis quickly looked away, focusing on the mess of bottles on the table instead.

"Guess I'll see you tomorrow," Tyler said, his voice low and warm.

"Yeah," Louis replied, trying to keep his tone casual despite the flutter in his chest.

Whilst the group dispersed and everyone headed up to their dorms, Louis couldn't help but feel a small buzz of anticipation. Tomorrow promised to be a day worth remembering.

As Louis settled into his bunk bed, the night's events replayed in his mind. The laughter, the conversations, and most of all, Tyler. He stared up at the ceiling, feeling the slight sway of the hostel bunk as someone shifted in the bed above him.

His phone buzzed on the small shelf by his bed. Reaching for it, he unlocked the screen to find a message from Tyler on Instagram:

Hey, had a good time tonight. See you tomorrow.

A smile crept onto Louis's face as he quickly typed a reply:

Same here! Looking forward to it x

He stared at the message, debating if the kiss was too much. Before he could overthink it, the notification of Tyler's reply appeared.

Cool, night, man. Don't stay up too late! X

Louis blushed, giggling softly to himself.

Night, man. You too X

Feeling lighter than he had in weeks, Louis placed his phone back on the shelf and lay back, a small smile still lingering as he stared at the ceiling. Tomorrow was already shaping up to be a good day.

The sunlight shone through the small gap in the curtains as Louis stirred awake. He stretched, groaning softly before pulling himself out of bed. The day stretched ahead of him, full of promise and if things went well, something more.

233

He quickly showered, the cool water refreshing as he planned his outfit in his head: black cargos, a clean white t-shirt, and his favourite, blue-striped quarter-zip. The look was casual but put-together, just how he liked it.

With his hair fixed and his essentials—wallet, phone, and water bottle—in his bag, Louis headed to the hostel lobby to meet Tyler. The American was already there, leaning casually against the wall, scrolling on his phone. His blonde hair caught the light from the nearby window, and his easy smile lit up when he noticed Louis.

"Hey, ready to go?" Tyler asked.

"Definitely," Louis replied, his nerves settling a little under Tyler's relaxed energy.

They hopped on the Tube to Westminster, chatting lightly as the train sped through the tunnels. When they emerged into the city, Big Ben loomed tall against the clear blue sky. Tyler paused, taking it in with an impressed whistle.

"It's even cooler in person," Tyler said, pulling out his phone. "Mind if I get a photo of you with it?"

Louis laughed, pretending to strike a dramatic pose. Tyler rolled his eyes but grinned as he snapped the picture. "Okay, now one where you don't look like you're auditioning for a soap opera."

They both laughed, settling for silly selfies and more candid shots before making their way toward the river.

"I've got an idea," Louis said, leading Tyler to the dock where the boats departed for Tower Bridge. "Fancy a ride?"

"Absolutely," Tyler said, his excitement evident.

Onboard, they found seats near the side, the cool breeze from the water a welcome reprieve from the heat. They sat close together, their arms brushing occasionally as they pointed out landmarks and joked about their lack of nautical knowledge. The conversation flowed easily, and Louis couldn't help but feel the growing pull of his attraction to Tyler.

When they disembarked near Tower Bridge, the afternoon unfolded in a perfect blend of sightseeing and relaxed exploration. They admired the grandeur of the Tower of London, joked about how Tyler would've fit right in as a knight, and marvelled at the architectural beauty of Tower Bridge.

Their next stop was the Tower Bridge Arms, a cosy pub where they ordered pints and shared a platter of pub classics: chips, mini sausages, and scotch eggs. The relaxed atmosphere gave Louis the courage to tease Tyler about his lack of knowledge about British food.

"What's a scotch egg?" Tyler had asked, looking genuinely puzzled.

"It's like an egg in armour," Louis joked.

"Like me—a knight," Tyler quipped, making them laugh.

As the day transitioned to evening, they walked toward The Shard, admiring the towering glass structure. Tyler couldn't resist snapping a few photos, while Louis admired the way the sunset reflected off its surface.

The train ride back to Pimlico was quieter, the hum of the train filling the silence between them. Tyler finally broke it, turning to Louis.

"So, tomorrow I'm heading to Paris at 7 am."

The words hit Louis harder than he expected. His chest tightened, and he forced a smile. "That's cool. Bet it'll be amazing."

"Yeah," Tyler said, though his tone sounded more thoughtful. "It's weird. I've been travelling solo for weeks, but this has been one of my favourite days."

Louis felt his heart race at the admission but tried to play it cool. "Same here," he said honestly.

As they neared Pimlico, Louis hesitated before speaking again. "There's one more place I'd love to see, and it's only about a ten-minute walk from the hostel. It's kind of a nerdy thing, but…

Tyler looked intrigued. "Go on."

"Battersea Power Station," Louis said, his face lighting up. "It was in Doctor Who. I've always wanted to see it, and I'd love to take you before you go."

Tyler's smile was immediate. "Sounds awesome. Let's do it."

Louis felt a flicker of hope as they stepped off the train. The day wasn't over yet, and, just maybe, there was still time for something more to happen.

Back at the hostel, Louis and Tyler cracked open a couple of their leftover drinks from the night before. The kitchen was quiet now, the hum of the refrigerator filling the space as they sat at one of the small tables.

"So," Louis asked, tipping his bottle toward Tyler, "what's one song that always gets you?"

Tyler did not even hesitate. "Piano Man by Billy Joel. My Da used to play it all the time when I was a kid. It's stuck with me."

Louis smiled, liking the idea of seeing Tyler hearing that song for the first time. "Good choice," he said. "It's a classic."

Feeling a little bold, Louis stood up and said, "Stay here. I'm making dinner."

Tyler raised an eyebrow. "You don't have to do that."

"Shush," Louis replied, opening the hostel pantry where spaghetti and canned tomatoes were stored. "I'm not letting you leave London without trying my spaghetti Bolognese. Sit tight."

As the pasta boiled and the rich scent of garlic and tomato sauce filled the air, Tyler leaned back in his chair, sipping his drink and watching Louis move around the kitchen.

"This smells amazing," Tyler said as Louis plated up two portions and set them on the table.

"Taste it first," Louis teased, sitting across from him.

Tyler twirled a forkful of spaghetti, took a bite, and gave an exaggerated groan of appreciation. "Okay, you're officially my favourite person in London right now."

Louis chuckled, his cheeks warming. They ate and talked, the conversation ranging from music to travel to their favourite childhood meals. Louis couldn't help but feel a pang of sadness knowing Tyler was leaving tomorrow, but he pushed it aside.

By 7 PM, the day was cooling into a perfect evening. Louis cleared their plates and said, "Come on, we're going to the power station now."

When they left the hostel, they stopped at a small shop near the station. Louis entered, asking for a packet of cigarettes and a clipper from the man behind counter. He paid, then stuffed them into his pocket.

"Didn't peg you for a smoker," Tyler said as they stepped back into the street.

"I'm not," Louis replied with a grin. "But on a night like this, it'd be rude not to."

They walked along the quiet streets toward Vauxhall, the glow of streetlights casting long shadows on the pavement. Louis lit a cigarette, inhaled, and then passed the pack to Tyler, who took one with a grin.

"This feels like a movie," Tyler said, blowing out a thin trail of smoke.

Louis laughed; the sound soft in the stillness of the night. "Wait," he said, fishing his phone from his pocket. "You said you liked Piano Man, right?"

He found the song and pressed play, the familiar piano chords floating into the air as they walked.

Tyler laughed. "No way. You're full of surprises, aren't you?"

As they strolled through the quiet streets, the two of them sang along, their slightly tipsy voices blending with the music. The city around them faded, and for a moment, it was just them, the song, and the cool evening air.

They crossed a road, the hum of the city blending with the distant sound of the Thames lapping against the bank. They paused at a wrought-iron fence that lined the river, the cool metal grounding them as they leaned against it, gazing across the water in wonder. The soft notes of "Piano Man" floated from Louis's phone, creating a nostalgic backdrop that wrapped around them like a familiar blanket.

"Battersea Power Station," Louis whispered, his voice barely above the sound of the flowing river. "One big Cyberman factory," he added, laughter spilling into the warm night air.

With an exaggerated roll of his eyes, Tyler took one last puff of his cigarette before flicking the butt into the Thames. The glowing ember plopped into the water, sending tiny ripples across the surface. "You're such a nerd! What's so special about Doctor Who?"

Louis turned his gaze back to the iconic structure, its massive silhouette bathed in the soft glow of lights flickering against the night sky. The four chimneys stood tall, like ancient sentinels guarding the secrets of the river. He felt a surge of emotion welling up inside him.

"It's got me through a lot," he said, his voice trembling slightly as he wrestled with the memories. "Being here just reminds me of the joy I felt watching it as a kid."

A wistful smile flickered across his face, but his eyes glistened with unshed tears. The weight of nostalgia mixed with sadness was palpable, pulling him into a vortex of days marked by loneliness and uncertainty, overshadowing the innocence he once cherished.

Sensing the shift in the atmosphere, Tyler wrapped an arm around Louis's shoulders, offering a comforting squeeze. They stood together in silence, gazing at the river. The distant sounds of the city created a soothing backdrop, blending seamlessly with the melody of the piano flowing from Louis's phone.

Breaking the silence, Louis took a deep breath, filling his lungs with the cool air. He reached into his pocket and pulled out the cigarettes, offering one to Tyler. They both lit up, the soft hiss of flames briefly illuminating their faces. As Louis inhaled deeply, he let the smoke linger, allowing it to rise and mix with the soft notes of the music enveloping them.

"It's just…" he began, his voice low, the rhythm of the city fading into the background. "Four years ago, I came down to London alone, just eighteen, filled with hope and dreams. I was convinced I had a bright future ahead of me. I was here for a piece for my blog, and I even interviewed an actor named Nicholas Briggs from Doctor Who. That year brought a lot of changes—some mistakes too—and I kind of stopped chasing my dreams. Being back here makes me reflect on everything I could've done, everything I could've become."

He paused, exhaling slowly, watching the smoke swirl and vanish into the night. "Honestly, I wouldn't even be standing here right now if it weren't for my Mum and my Gran. I don't think I'd still be alive without them. But here I am, and I'm proud of how much I've grown over the years."

They both finished their cigarettes, their eyes drawn to the glowing embers in their hands. They let the embers fall into the Thames with a quiet resolve, watching as the tiny lights disappeared into the dark waters. The music swelled softly, echoing the bittersweet notes of Louis's reflection as they stood together, united in the moment.

Tyler leaned off the railing, turning to face Louis as their eyes locked. The music faded out, leaving an intimate silence between them. At that moment, Tyler looked striking, illuminated by the moonlight. His features were sharp and youthful, reminiscent of a young Leonardo DiCaprio. Louis felt his heart quicken, a mix of longing and vulnerability washing over him.

"I'm really glad you're still here," Tyler said, sincerity lacing his words. "I'm glad I met you."

Feeling a rush of emotion, Louis leaned in to kiss Tyler, his heart racing with hope. But to his surprise, Tyler pulled away, leaving a knot of disappointment in Louis's stomach.

"But… I'm not gay," Tyler whispered, his voice soft yet firm, an apology hidden in the corners.

Louis's cheeks flushed with a mix of shame and hurt. "I'm sorry," he stammered, scrambling to find the right words. Before he could finish, Tyler reached out, grabbing him and pulling him into a long, warm embrace.

Tyler's arms wrapped around him, holding him close, offering comfort and an unexpected sense of safety. The world around them faded, leaving only the rhythmic heartbeat of the city and the warmth shared between them.

Louis smiled, resting his head on Tyler's shoulder, inhaling the scent of his wavy hair, which smelled faintly of shampoo and something uniquely him.

He chuckled softly, the tension easing slightly, buoyed by the unexpected intimacy of the moment. "God, I always fall for straight guys," he murmured playfully, his voice barely above a whisper as he nestled closer, grateful for the warmth of the embrace.

Tyler pulled back slightly, a teasing smile forming on his lips. "I don't blame you," he joked, his eyes sparkling. Then he nodded toward the darkened streets ahead, where the soft glow of streetlights beckoned. "Come on, let's get back to the hostel."

They turned away from the power station, beginning to walk back the way they came. The vibrant energy of London's nightlife surrounded them, the sounds of laughter and conversation spilling from nearby pubs, intertwining with the distant music echoes. As they strolled through the nighttime streets, the city thrummed with life, each step feeling lighter, as if the weight of the past was slowly lifting, leaving space for the promise of what could be.

With each stride, Louis felt a flicker of hope reigniting within him, fuelled by the sudden friendship he shared with Tyler and the memories they had created together. The Thames whispered its secrets as they walked, and at that, amidst the hustle and bustle of London, everything felt possible again.

Louis woke up slowly; he rubbed his eyes, feeling the weight of the day ahead pressing on his chest. He checked the time: 10am. He had missed saying his goodbyes. Tyler had left for Paris.

A pang of sadness twisted in Louis's stomach as he reached for his phone. Typing out a quick message, he wished Tyler luck on his journey:

Good luck in Paris Mr Piano Man. Hope it's everything you dreamed of."

Tyler's reply came instantly:

Thanks, Billy Joel. I'll miss you. Take care of yourself Louis.

Louis smiled, a bittersweet feeling washing over him. There was something about this trip, this time in London, which had changed him. Maybe it was the people he had met, or maybe it was the city itself—so full of energy, history, and dreams. He tucked his phone back into his pocket and got dressed.

He went downstairs for breakfast, where Stella was already seated, waiting with a plate of toast. She looked up and waved as he approached, her smile warm and inviting.

"Morning," she said, gesturing to the seat across from her. "How did you sleep?"

"Not great," Louis admitted, sitting down and grabbing a piece of toast. "Tyler's gone. I think it hit me more than I expected."

Stella nodded sympathetically. "I can imagine. It's always tough when people leave. But hey, I'm still here," she winked.

Louis chuckled, taking a bite of his toast. The warmth of Stella's company made the morning feel a little brighter. They chatted casually about the previous night, and before long, Stella brought up the idea of going to Camden Market.

"How about we head to Camden today?" she suggested. "It'll be a nice way to spend the day. I can show you around."

Louis thought about it for a minute before nodding. "Yeah, sounds great."

They finished their breakfast and set out for Camden, strolling through the markets, weaving in and out of stalls filled with vintage clothes, quirky trinkets, and mouthwatering food. The atmosphere was buzzing with excitement, and Louis found himself caught up in it, his mind temporarily distracted from the sadness of leaving tomorrow. They had food from a stall, savouring the flavours and enjoying his last day.

As they walked, Louis felt a sense of realisation. "I'm leaving tomorrow morning," he said quietly, glancing at Stella. "Heading home."

Stella's expression softened, and she reached out, giving his arm a gentle squeeze. "I'll miss you," she said, her voice tinged with sadness. "But you know, you'll always have somewhere to stay if you ever come to Australia."

Louis smiled, touched by her words. "Thanks, Stella. It means a lot."

They kept walking, and Louis paused, staring at the bustling scene around him. "You know," he began, his voice thoughtful, "I dream of living in London one day. Being here has made me realise how much is out there... How much is beyond the horizon."

Stella smiled, her eyes reflecting a mixture of understanding and longing. "I get that. There's something special about this city. It's like it has its heartbeat; you know? And it's so easy to get lost in it."

245

Louis nodded, feeling the weight of those words. "Yeah. Maybe one day I'll be back, for good."

As the afternoon sun began to dip, they decided to rent Lime bikes, and what followed was pure, unfiltered fun. They zoomed through the streets, laughing at the occasional wobble or near-miss, the freedom of the moment filling them with joy.

By the time they returned to the hostel, they were both a little out of breath but smiling, the joy of the ride lingering between them. They had dinner together, laughing over silly stories and talking about their respective lives. Later, they watched a bit of television, the hum of the hostel in the background as the evening wore on.

When the time came for Louis to pack, he did so slowly, as though trying to stretch out the hours before he left. Stella helped him with the last of his things, and they shared a quiet goodbye before Louis headed to bed. The pillow felt unusually soft that night, the weight of the journey home hanging heavy in the air.

He woke early as the sun was just beginning to rise. He said his goodbyes to Stela, before leaving the hostel – and the memories he had made here- behind. He made his way to Victoria Coach Station, the familiar sights triggering a rush of memories. This was where it all began—where his bus arrived all those years ago for his interview. The feeling of possibility, of uncertainty, had been so strong then. Now, it was a little different. The hope was still there, but it was tempered with a quiet knowing that life had a way of pushing forward, no matter how much you wished to hold onto certain moments.

He boarded the bus to Stansted Airport, settling into his seat. The journey back home felt surreal, the city already beginning to fade into the distance. As the bus pulled away, Louis promised himself one thing: I'll be back one day. And next time, it will be for good.

The horizon was waiting—his horizon.

CHAPTER FIFTEEN
HOMECOMING

A few days had passed since Louis returned home, and as he stood in his flat, he felt a strange mix of emotions. He had arrived back to the quiet of his one-bedroom apartment, the bustling energy of London still echoing in his mind. Now, sitting on his couch, the city felt like a distant dream, yet the lessons he had learned there were still vivid, still alive inside him.

Today, he had invited his Mum and Gran over. They had been eager to hear about his trip, and he was excited to share every detail, showing them how much the experience had meant to him. The doorbell rang, and he rushed to answer, greeted by the familiar faces of his mum and Gran.

"Hello, love," Mum said with a smile, stepping inside, her eyes scanning the room with a warm familiarity. "We missed you."

Gran followed close behind, her face lighting up as she took in the sight of the flat. "It's looking great, Louis," she said, her voice filled with pride. "You've made it your own."

"Thanks, Gran," Louis replied, leading them into the living room. "I've been busy with little projects here and there." He smiled, gesturing around the space, but his mind was elsewhere—on his trip and how it had changed him.

They sat down, and Louis started recounting his adventure, his voice animated as he described his time in London. "Honestly, it was incredible," he said, his eyes alight with the memories. "The markets, the people, the energy... It opened my eyes. I've never felt more alive like I was where I was meant to be."

Mum listened intently, her face softening with each word. She had always known Louis had a thirst for something bigger. "I'm so glad you went, Louis," she said. "You deserve to see the world, to experience these things."

Louis paused, feeling a lump form in his throat. "I do, Mum. I never realised how much I was holding back until I went there. I'm so grateful you helped me make it happen. It's changed my life."

Gran smiled warmly, reaching for his hand. "You've come a long way, son," she said, her voice filled with tenderness. "I'm proud of you."

Louis's heart swelled at her words. It had been a long journey, filled with ups and downs, but at this moment, sitting here with his Mum and Gran, he felt a sense of peace he hadn't known in a long time.

"Now, enough of all this talk," Mum said with a grin. "Let's have some dinner, yeah? I've made your favourite."

Louis's stomach rumbled in response, and he followed them to the small kitchen where his Mum had prepared his favourite - macaroni mince. The smell of it filled the room, and Louis couldn't help but feel a sense of comfort in the familiar flavours. They sat down together, digging in and laughing over stories of his trip, the conversation flowing effortlessly as it always did when they were together.

After dinner, they lingered at the table, chatting about small things—work, family, plans. But as the evening wore on, Louis felt a subtle shift. He could sense that the time to say goodbye was approaching.

"Well, we'd better get going," his Mum said, standing and hugging him. "It's getting late."

Gran followed suit, pulling him into a warm embrace. "You know we're always here for you, Louis," she said softly. "You're doing amazing. Don't ever forget that."

Louis smiled; his heart full. "I won't, Gran. Thanks for everything."

As they left, the door closed softly behind them, and Louis stood there momentarily, letting the silence settle around him. The apartment felt emptier without them, but he didn't mind. He was learning to find peace in the quiet, in the space he had carved out for himself. He had come a long way, and though the road ahead was uncertain, he felt ready for whatever came next for the first time in a long time.

He returned to the kitchen, rinsing off his plate and setting it aside before glancing around the room. This was his life now. And it was more than enough.

A new chapter had begun, and it was his to write.

The night had settled in, and the soft hum of the town outside was the only sound that filled Louis's flat. The glow of his laptop screen illuminated his face as he sat on his couch, his eyes scanning through different job listings in London. His fingers hovered over the keyboard, uncertain. There were plenty of options, but nothing felt right just yet. He clicked on a few links and browsed through some positions in journalism, his heart racing with anticipation and doubt.

He had decided to stay home for now, to settle in and take things slow, but the pull of London—the city that had reawakened something inside him—was undeniable. It was a place where dreams seemed within reach, where he could finally build the life, he had always wanted. But what would it take to get there? What steps would he need to take to make that dream real?

Louis leaned back on his sofa, staring at the screen. He felt a strange frustration, not with the process, but with himself. He wanted to do so much, but it felt like there was still so much standing in his way. He ran a hand through his hair, then closed his laptop, the quiet click of the lid closing filling the room.

A thought crept into his mind, something brewing for a while now. He pulled out his phone and opened the camera app. The idea of documenting this moment—capturing his thoughts, feelings, and the uncertainty that clung to him like a shadow—felt oddly comforting.

With a deep breath, he tapped record. The screen blinked to life, and Louis stared into the lens, unsure of what he was about to say.

"Okay," he started, his voice sounding softer than expected. "This feels strange, but… I want to do something. I want to record this moment. Not for anyone else, just for me. So that in a year, I can look back and see how far I've come."

He shifted on his sofa, feeling a mix of vulnerability and hope. "I've just gotten back from London; honestly, it's changed me. It's made me realise how much more there is to life—so much I still want to see, so much I still want to do. I keep thinking about how close I am and how far away I feel. I'm standing on the edge of something big, but I'm unsure how to take the first step."

Louis paused, his eyes drifting to the window, where the city lights flickered in the distance. "I don't know what the future holds, but I'm trying to figure it out. And I think that's enough for now. I've got to believe it is. Just take it day by day, right?"

He looked back at the camera, his face grave but determined. "One day, I'll be back in London. I'll have made it as a writer. When that day comes, I want to look back on this and remember what it felt like at that moment. The uncertainty, the dreams, the hope."

Louis chuckled softly, shaking his head. "Anyway, that's it for tonight. I just needed to get this off my chest. I'll see where I am in a year. Hopefully, things will be different. Hopefully, they'll be better."

He stopped the recording and sat in silence for a moment, watching the screen go black. It felt almost cathartic to put his thoughts into words and take a step toward something he couldn't quite define yet. Maybe he wasn't ready for the big moves just yet, but this small act of recording his thoughts felt like a start.

Louis leaned back on his couch, a small smile tugging at the corner of his lips. He didn't know exactly where this journey would take him, but for the first time in a long time, he felt he was on the right path.

The night had grown quieter, the stillness that only came in the late hours when the world seemed to exhale. Louis sat on his worn sofa, the soft flicker of a candle casting warm light across the walls. His cat, Hope, was perched on his lap, her velvety purring a comforting rhythm against the silence.

He stroked her absentmindedly, her sleek fur soothingly under his fingers. Hope had been with him through the past year, a constant companion in the solitude of his flat. He hadn't named her; her name was already Hope, but now, the name seemed more fitting than ever.

Louis glanced around the room. It wasn't much—just a tiny one-bedroom flat with thrifted furniture and his personal touches scattered about—but it was his. It represented independence, growth, and a journey he was still navigating.

The buzz of his phone broke the silence, the screen lighting up with a name that tightened his chest: *Dad.*

Louis just stared at the screen for a moment, his heart pounding. It had been years since they'd spoken years filled with silence and distance. He wasn't sure what had caused his Dad to call now, but he knew he couldn't let it go unanswered.

With a deep breath, he swiped to answer and brought the phone to his ear.

"Hi, Dad," he said, his voice steady but laced with emotion.

There was a pause on the other end, just long enough for the moment's weight to settle between them.

"Hi, Louis," his Dad finally replied, his voice softer than Louis remembered. "I... I just wanted to check-in. See how you're doing."

Hope shifted on his lap, curling up tighter as if sensing the moment's importance. Louis smiled faintly, running a hand over her back as he leaned into the conversation.

"I'm okay," Louis said, glancing around his flat. "Actually... I'm doing better than I have in a while."

The words felt authentic, and as he said them, a sense of peace washed over him. He wasn't where he wanted to be, but he was on his way. And in this small flat, with Hope perched on his lap and his Dad's voice on the other end of the line, he realised he had something he hadn't had in a long time: a sense of hope.

It wasn't a grand moment, not the ending he'd ever imagined, but it felt right. This was his life—imperfect, evolving, and filled with possibilities.

Louis leaned back, letting the conversation unfold, feeling the weight of the past begin to lift. The future was still unwritten, but for the first time in a long time, he was excited to see where it would lead.

And as the night stretched on, Louis sat there with Hope on his lap and a quiet smile on his face, knowing that sometimes, endings weren't endings at all. *They were just new beginnings waiting to be written.*

Behind the Horizon (An afterwards) ...

In 2020, I turned 18 years old while studying Journalism and Radio at a college in Glasgow. Back then, we'd all heard about COVID, but none of us could have imagined the strain it would bring to the country and our lives. Like most 18-year-olds, I frequently went on nights out with my close friend group. I dabbled in party drugs, but at the time, I thought of it as something everyone my age did—just harmless fun. I loved studying. I loved writing. I interviewed many actors, such as Katy Manning, Nicholas Briggs, Sophie Aldred, Tara Ward, and Anjili Mohindra—all from Doctor Who, of course. I attended press events for my blog, and I was even invited to the Still Game premiere of the final series, which I attended with my big brother Ally, a lifelong fan.

After turning 18, I was most looking forward to an apprenticeship I had secured at the BBC that summer, thinking it would propel me further in my journalism career. However, when COVID finally arrived, this was soon put on hold. The pandemic battered the country—and it battered my mental health. I'm a people person through and through. Anyone who knows me will tell you I love to talk, make people laugh, and thrive when I'm surrounded by loved ones. So, with isolation and being around only my Mum, who was also grappling with her mental health struggles after a separation and the absence of my youngest brother (through no fault of her own), my mental health deteriorated rapidly.

Then, the passing of my beloved childhood dog, Mika, struck a deep chord. My Mum and I both spiralled into a shared depression. As restrictions eased, I did what many my age were doing—going on drives with friends and hitting the nightlife scene. But the drugs became more frequent on these nights out. They seemed to make the world just a bit brighter amidst the uncertainty COVID-19 had brought.

When my grandmother died, it plunged me further into despair. I hadn't seen her for at least two years before her passing, which left me with an overwhelming sense of guilt and loss. In my grief, I began seeking validation and attention from boys on nights out or on Grindr, which often left me heartbroken and even more vulnerable.

In this book, I mention a memory box—the same memory box I still have now, tucked under the bed in my one-bedroom apartment. Louis's story is deeply rooted in my own experiences, and if you've read the book rather than skipping to the back, you'll have reached the point where Louis, in his darkest moment, looks through the memories in that shoebox and tries to overdose. This is a moment taken directly from my life—something I've rarely shared with anyone outside close friends and family. I can only urge anyone who has ever felt that way, or who is feeling that way now, to seek help. Reach out to Samaritans or a mental health practitioner. The world is a better place with you in it, and things do get better.

A few months after this low point, I moved into my flat, gaining independence and creating a space for myself. It was the best decision I could have made. Since then, I've travelled to Paris and London, met amazing people, seen Taylor Swift live (an absolute highlight), and grown closer to incredible friends. Life is so much more than the pain you're feeling now. There is always hope beyond the horizon.

I'd like to take this moment to thank my Mum and Gran, who have been my rocks through thick and thin. A special mention also goes to my 'Karen'—she knows who she is. Karen is a friend I gained during the year of COVID-19, and she's been my best friend ever since. We've helped each other through our darkest days with our little jokes, and silly dances, and shared love for songs like "Enjoy the Silence," "Hometown Glory," and Kylie Minogue's "Can't Get You Out of My Head."

Lastly, I want to dedicate this to Karen's Dad, who sadly passed away. Thank you for raising such a beautiful, kind-hearted person who has been a lifeline to me in times of uncertainty.

Now, as I write this, I am 23 years old. This year, I am focusing on forging a new mindset, improving my mental health, and working on my fitness to be the best version of myself. Writing this book and reliving my past was emotionally taxing, but it also showed me how far I've come. I strive every day to become the best Blair I can be—the best Louis I can be. Louis was created to tell my story, and he will forever hold a special place in my heart.

As I close this chapter, I feel a renewed sense of purpose and a deep gratitude for the journey that brought me here.

Thank you for reading and for being a part of my story

"Life depends on change and renewal".

The Second Doctor
Doctor Who

WHATS NEXT FROM BLAIR LINDSAY?

On the horizon is a series I have titled The Buchanan Bureau. A gripping spy thriller set in the heart of Scotland. The story follows an elite intelligence team navigating a web of secrets, deception, and danger as they race to uncover a conspiracy threatening national security. Packed with twists, intrigue, and complex characters, this novel delves into the moral complexities of espionage and the fine line between loyalty and betrayal., is a thrilling spy novel that explores mystery, betrayal, and the strength of trust in the most uncertain of times. It's a very different kind of story, but one I'm equally passionate about. I hope you'll join me for that adventure as well.

COVER TO BE CONFIRMED...

THE BUCHANAN BUREAU – A NATION BETRAYED

In the heart of Glasgow, hidden within the iconic Lighthouse building, lies the Buchanan Bureau, the UK's last line of defence against chaos. Fraser Galloway, a skilled agent and devoted patriot, balances his high-stakes career with a loving relationship with his Russian boyfriend, Dimitri Romanov. But Fraser's world is shattered on the night of their anniversary when a devastating explosion destroys Glasgow's City Chambers— and similar attacks strike key government sites across the UK.

As the chaos spreads, the next targets are clear: police stations and MI5 buildings in London, Glasgow, Cardiff, and Belfast. With communication networks severed and the police force crippled, the Buchanan Bureau becomes the only agency capable of coordinating a response. But when Russia claims responsibility for the attacks, suspicion falls on Dimitri, forcing Fraser to question the man he loves.

While Fraser works tirelessly with allied intelligence bureaus to stop the escalating threat, Russian troops begin entering UK airspace undetected, leaving cities vulnerable and plunging the nation into chaos. As soldiers roll out into the streets and fear grips the public, Fraser must navigate mounting tension and impossible choices.

With the UK teetering on the brink of World War III, Fraser is determined to protect his country and uncover the truth. But in a world of secrets and lies, the line between friend and foe begins to blur, leaving Fraser to face challenges that will test his loyalty, courage, and resolve.

COMING SOON …

ENJOYED THE BOOK?

If you enjoyed the book, I would be incredibly grateful if you could share your thoughts with others. Your thoughts help others discover *Beyond the Horizon* and allows me to grow as a writer. Whether it is a few words or a detailed reflection, your feedback means the world to me.

You can leave a review on:

- Amazon
- Goodreads

Your support not only helps independent authors like me but also encourages us to keep telling stories that matter.

Thank you again for joining Louis on his journey. I hope this is just the beginning of many stories we will share together. And remember – there is always hope *beyond the horizon.*

Blair
Lindsay

Printed in Great Britain
by Amazon

57759524R00152